FAITH LIKE POTATOES

FAITH
LIKE
POTATOES

The story of a farmer
who risked everything for God

ANGUS BUCHAN
with
Jan Greenough and Val Waldeck

MONARCH
BOOKS
Oxford, UK & Grand Rapids, Michigan, USA

First published in South Africa in 1998.
This edition first published in the UK in 2006 by Monarch Books
(a publishing imprint of Lion Hudson plc),
Mayfield House, 256 Banbury Road, Oxford OX2 7DH
Tel: +44 (0) 1865 302750   Fax: +44 (0) 1865 302757
Email: monarch@lionhudson.com
www.lionhudson.com

Reprinted 2006

Distributed by:
UK: Marston Book Services Ltd, PO Box 269,
Abingdon, Oxon OX14 4YN
USA: Kregel Publications, PO Box 2607,
Grand Rapids, Michigan 49501.

ISBN-13: 978-1-85424-740-7 (UK)
ISBN-10: 1-85424-740-9 (UK)
ISBN-13: 978-0-8254-6111-8 (USA)
ISBN-10: 0-8254-6111-1 (USA)

Contents

Acknowledgements

To Jan Greenough, and Val Waldeck for helping me capture the story on paper.

Yvonne Ashwell, for all the typing.
Clive Thompson for the photography.
Tony Collins for his encouragement, and godly counsel.

For all those wonderful folk who have walked this road with Jill and I, and made the story possible!

1
Faith Like Potatoes

"*T*o hell with El Niño!"

I looked out over the vast crowds gathered in King's Park Rugby Stadium, and I knew I had their full attention.

"To hell with the drought warnings and the fear and the worry! We are not listening to the lies of the devil. We are listening to the promises of God!"

My audience looked at me in stunned silence. They had come to Durban in September 1997 for the Peace Gathering hosted by Shalom Ministries, and they knew weather as only farmers can: they knew it could make or break them.

El Niño comes around every three to seven years. A warm current of water in the Eastern Pacific triggers unusual weather conditions around the world, bringing torrential rain in some places and extended periods of drought in others – Southern Africa in particular. That year all the signs were that El Niño was the strongest for 50 years, and the drought would be correspondingly worse. The newspapers, TV and radio seemed to talk about nothing else. Even the Agricultural Union had succumbed to the current fears.

"Don't plant expensive crops," they advised. "Keep your outlay to a minimum. Plant only the crops you know will grow. This is going to be a drought year, so it's a year to consolidate."

The audience in front of me knew that. They knew I was a farmer, too, so they could hardly believe that I was serious.

"This year we are going to plant potatoes! We are going back and we're going to plant all our lands – every square inch of ground – with mealies and dry beans and potatoes. We are going to trust God for our needs!"

That night as I drove home I wondered if I was being rash. "Me and my big mouth," I thought. "If this isn't really God's will, I'm in real trouble this time." If I was wrong, it could mean the loss of my entire farm. I prayed earnestly: "Guide me, Lord. I need a specific direction from you now."

Sure enough, the conviction came into my heart: I was to plant ten hectares of potatoes. "OK, Lord, I'll do it," I said. "Ten hectares it shall be." I was filled with determination to believe God whatever the cost. It was all or nothing.

Planting potatoes is a very expensive exercise, as any farmer knows. In addition to the cost of the seed potatoes, there is also the extra fertiliser. When you plant mealies (known as maize or sweetcorn in the UK) you only put down about 350 to 400 kilos of fertiliser per hectare, but potatoes need at least a tonne. The spray programme to keep blight at bay costs about 6,000 Rand (around £500). Add in the cost of labour and you begin to understand that planting potatoes is a big investment – it isn't what you do when you're being cautious.

My neighbouring farmers were horrified. "Listen, Angus," said one. "I've heard you're planning to put in potatoes. Please don't do it ... it'll be the finish of you. I've seen too many farms go bankrupt. You've been around here for 20 years and we don't want to lose you. Why not try broiler chicks or something else?"

"I have to do it," I replied. "I have to do what God has told me to."

"But you've never planted potatoes before. You've got no experience. You've got no irrigation. The biggest drought in history is on the way. Don't do it!"

I couldn't be persuaded, though it was near the end of the planting season, and I knew it was going to be difficult to find the seed. You actually plant potatoes to get potatoes, and what we eventually found wasn't the best. The bags were so rotten that when we picked them up the seed potatoes fell out, and we saw that shoots had already begun to grow. Still, we bought up everything we could find, and we planted it all. Six lorry-loads of seed potatoes went into those ten hectares of ground.

We planted up the rest of the farm, too, with the mealies and the dry beans, but it was the potatoes that concerned us most – they represented such a big investment. Potatoes need a lot of water, because they are 90 per cent water themselves, and that drought was a real test of my faith. Sometimes it would begin to rain, and our spirits would rise – then it would stop, everything would become dry and dusty, and the devil would accuse me. "You've got yourself in real trouble now! Where is the money going to come from this year?" He never missed an opportunity to taunt me, and we had to walk by faith every step of the way.

Normally, in a drought year, farmers plant with minimum fertiliser, minimum cost, minimum everything. And of course, they get only a minimum return. One of my neighbours planted only soya beans, a low-input crop requiring little moisture, and a safe bet for a drought year. But he didn't make much profit: soya beans also give the farmer a low return. That makes sense. The Lord says, "Whoever sows sparingly will also reap sparingly, and whoever sows generously will also reap generously" (2 Corinthians 9:6).

My friends Jeff, Peter and Dieter, fellow believers and local farmers, knew a lot about potatoes, and they came over every day to check on the crop. Did we baby those potatoes! We sprayed them, we kept them clean, we gave them the Rolls-Royce treatment. Everyone looked on in amazement, but we were trusting God.

Meanwhile, Christians all over the country had heard about my crop and were praying for it. I wondered if I should make a few contingency plans. I had no irrigation equipment so I asked a local farmer to lend me a couple of pipes to attach to my borehole, to give me a chance of getting some extra water. He gave me twelve sprays – not nearly enough to get around ten hectares of land. I was back to relying on God, and he never let us down. Every time the land looked too dry, I would connect the pipes and switch on the sprays – and down would come the rain, so I had to switch off the water and apologise to God! That happened over and over again: the Lord watched over those plants every inch of the way.

It was the first time I had ever grown potatoes, so I wasn't quite sure what to expect. However, when we began harvesting, the experts told me that I had a bumper crop. Those potatoes were the best in the country. In fact, they were just about the only ones in the country, because most other farmers had been scared off from planting them. There was a general shortage, so we had no trouble selling our miracle potatoes at a good price.

There's a care home for the elderly near my farm, and I often speak there. Every time I visited that year, the old folk wanted to know how the crops were faring. One day I dug up some really big potatoes, washed them and put them in a bag with some mealies. When I finished preaching, I took them out and put them on the table. "This is what Jesus has done," I said. "This is the way he has rewarded our faith. Our God is the God of the impossible, and El Niño has no power like his."

Many of the labourers on our farm were Christians, and they usually had to put up with a great deal of mockery from their friends for standing up for Christ. Now they had an answer. "Where is this El Niño the clever people tell us about every day on the radio?" they asked. "Now you can see for yourself that we serve the living God."

Those potatoes caught the imagination of Christians all over the country. I spoke to a group of black pastors in Magaliesberg one day, and they said, "Every time we eat a potato from now on, we will remember this: 'Without faith it is impossible to please God, because anyone who comes to him must believe that he exists and that he rewards those who earnestly seek him'" (Hebrews 11:6).

Peter Marshall, the great evangelical preacher, once said that we need "faith like potatoes" – plain, simple, real faith that will sustain us in our everyday lives. Whenever I pick up a potato I remember those words. That's the kind of faith I want. When we have faith and act on it, God will come through for us, no matter what our circumstances. God is King!

2
The Road to Shalom

I'm a real Scottish lad. My parents were both born in Aberdeenshire in Scotland, and my father, George Buchan, was a country blacksmith. He first came to South Africa just before the Second World War, when he was 18. When war broke out he joined the Transvaal Scottish Regiment, was captured in North Africa and spent the next three years in a German prisoner-of-war camp. On his release he returned to Scotland to marry my mother, and together they returned to Africa.

My brother and I were both born in Bulawayo, Southern Rhodesia (now called Zimbabwe). Later Mum and Dad decided to move to Ndola in Northern Rhodesia (now Zambia), where my sister was born and where we all grew up. That was where I first encountered Jesus.

I must have been six or seven years old at the time, and I had gone with a friend to the local cinema. There was no television in Zambia, so Saturday afternoon at the local bioscope, as we called it, was the social highlight of our week. We watched a film, and in the interval we kids would meet up, swap comics and make friends.

This particular day was different, however. There was a Billy Graham Crusade going on in a nearby town, and one of the workers had come to the cinema to preach. He must have presented his message well, because my young heart was gripped; when he asked us if we wanted to ask Jesus into our lives, I was one of the first to respond. I don't know how much I understood about it, but I knew I wanted to have that new life that he was talking about.

Many people wonder about the results of mass evangelism, and whether those who respond at meetings continue in the faith after the evangelist goes home. I know that when God does a real work in anyone's heart, something happens. That's why, whenever I preach, I always give people an opportunity to respond to God. The Bible says that you cannot call Jesus Christ Lord unless the Holy Spirit moves you; I defy anyone to pray the sinner's prayer – acknowledging their sin and asking Jesus to come into their life – without being touched by God.

My new faith made a real difference to my life, as young as I was. I started going to church – alone, because none of the family was at all interested in religion, and no one wanted to come with me. I used to cycle there every Sunday evening, and it became my job to tidy the church and lock up. There weren't many kids my age at the church, but I stayed on there because the people made me feel loved and welcomed. By the age of fifteen I was a Sunday School teacher, and at the age of 16 I preached my first sermon! It wasn't very long – about six and a half minutes – but it was a very exciting moment.

Dad didn't make it easy for me: he teased me unmercifully when I went to church or if he saw me reading the Bible my mum gave me. I tried to get him to come to church with me, but he wouldn't budge. I spent most of my teenage years trying to serve the Lord, but never quite getting there. The seed had been planted, but it would be many years before it began to germinate.

I grew up in a mining town, but I always knew that I wanted to be a farmer. I hadn't done too well at school, and I didn't get my matriculation certificate, only a school-leaving certificate for Standard Eight. I wanted to go to agricultural college, and my parents suggested that I might like to study in Scotland. It would be an opportunity to learn all the skills I needed, and at the same time to visit my grandparents and the rest of the family and get in touch with my Scottish roots.

I loved being in Scotland and felt at home there. My parents retained their Scottish accents to the end of their lives, so the voices I heard in Scotland sounded just like home to me.

I spent two great years at Craibstone Agricultural College, and I learned a lot. We were outside in all weathers – sleet, snow and rain – doing hard manual work, and it really toughened me up. The farmers of north-east Scotland are excellent stockmen, and I learned my livestock farming on the Aberdeen Angus cattle of the area. The dairy and arable farming I learned there has stood me in good stead to this day.

I tried going to church on Sundays but I found it dull – and besides, I was beginning to have other interests. In those days I didn't have much self-confidence, especially where girls were concerned: I was thin, spotty and knock-kneed – not a good start for a teenage boy. But the physical work was putting muscle on me, and the fresh air and good food cleared up my teenage skin. My confidence was improving. I went to the gym and started playing rugby; I was persuaded to go out with the rest of the boys for a few beers in the pub; I met girls and found I could talk to them without blushing. I was growing up, becoming popular, doing well – and slowly the attractions of the world were drawing me away from God. I thought I was happy, but like the prodigal son, I was in a far country, and I had lost touch with the Father.

When I graduated in 1968 I came home to Zambia and got a job on a farm in the copper belt. It was a good life: I was assistant manager on the farm, and had my own house. I made a couple of visits to my parents, but I was enjoying my independence as a "wild colonial boy" – there were lots of parties, lots of girlfriends and plenty of opportunities for drinking with the boys. My social life was great, but I was a long way from God. There is an emptiness in the heart of man that nothing but God himself can fill. St Augustine spoke of it as a "God-shaped space", and I knew it, though I didn't recognise it for what it was. I felt restless and unfulfilled, and I thought more travelling might be the answer.

I gave up my job and flew to Australia, making a beeline for Bondi Beach, where all the beautiful girls sunbathed. It was fantastic, but I couldn't afford to stay there for long. I needed a job, and there was plenty of farm work available for a fit young man who wasn't afraid of hard work. I worked on a dairy farm in Picton, New South Wales, milking cows; then I had a job on one of the top Hereford beef stud farms, where I rode horses and learned to break in the bulls for showing. I spent a term at Hawkesbury Agricultural College: they wanted me to stay because I was so good at rugby, but I wasn't cut out for academic life and I moved on again, this time to Queensland, where I harvested pineapples. Even there I made a success of it – three of us set a record by picking 17 tonnes of fruit in one day, though it was incredibly tough work, and at night we had to pick the thorns out of our hands by candlelight.

I'd made some good money, and I was used to living life at a fast pace: I was rich, independent and proud, but I still felt restless, and I didn't feel I had a future in Australia. My younger brother Fergus wrote to me saying that there were good opportunities in Zambia, so I sold my car and flew home to my beloved Africa.

Once there, I immediately found a good job as manager of a big farm in a place called Broken Hill: 4,000 hectares, 1,500 head of cattle and 130 workers. I increased in maturity and developed my leadership and farming skills, but I carried on with my usual lifestyle, drinking with the boys (and the girls), taking up competitive power-lifting, and glorying in my own success. I was an arrogant, successful, self-made man. However, God had his hand on my life, and sent me a great blessing: my wife Jill.

We met at a party, and it was love at first sight; two years later we married in the local magistrates' court. Jill is a real bush baby – she was born in Kasama, northern Zambia, where her English parents ran a centre for the treatment of leprosy. God has given me a wife who has a great love for farming, for Africa and the African people, and who stands beside me in all I do.

She supported me when I decided to leave my secure job and buy a farm in partnership with a friend, Jan "John Bull" Coetzee. It was a great opportunity, and when John Bull decided to move on I was able to buy him out and became the proud owner of a beautiful 1,500-hectare farm with a herd of 250 beef cattle and other stock. It was a hard life but a good one. I was working long hours clearing the bush, planting corn and building the herd of beef cattle. Jill was kept busy running the home and looking after the babies: our first son Andrew and our daughters Lindi and Robyn were born there.

It looked as though I was settling down at last, but God had other plans. Conditions in Zambia were deteriorating: the value of the currency was going down, medical care was hard to find and the educational system was poor. Andrew and Lindi were ready for school, but there was nowhere suitable nearby, and we were determined not to put our toddlers on a plane to England or South Africa, as so many other parents did. Jill had grown up in a boarding school and felt that she hardly knew her parents. She wanted us to be there for our children, and we're glad we made that decision. Today all five of them love the Lord and we are a very close family.

We agreed that we would have to move, but it was a bad time to sell up, and we handed over the farm for a fraction of its value. We lost money, and we would have to start all over again. In December 1976 we started packing up to leave.

"What shall we take with us?" the children asked.

"Everything we can fit in," we told them. We had a Mercedes Benz truck and trailer, and we filled it to capacity: a tractor, a lathe, welding machines, tools, furniture – it was amazing what we took. I drove the truck and Jill followed in the car with the children.

It was a hair-raising trip. The Victoria Falls road was blocked so we drove up-country towards Botswana, crossing the mighty Zambezi River on a pontoon bridge. The bush war in Rhodesia was at its height, and vehicles had to be escorted by armoured cars and jeeps with mounted machine guns. The recommended minimum speed through these war-torn areas was 120 kilometres per hour, but the truck would only do 60 kilometres per hour. Jill refused to go in a convoy without me, so she drove behind the truck all the way. I remember coming round a blind corner and seeing the security forces parked beside the road engaged in enemy contact: they had seen some terrorists about to attack our convoy, and soldiers were chasing them through the bush. We just kept driving.

Eventually we arrived in Swaziland, where I took a job on a farm. Neither of us was happy there. I found it hard to make the change from being self-employed to conforming to company regulations, working set hours and being told what jobs to do. Jill was also han-

kering for the independence and the wide open spaces
we were used to. Every six weeks we had a long weekend, and we would drive into South Africa to look for
a farm to buy. The prices were astronomical, and I
thought we would never be able to afford what we
wanted. We lowered our sights – maybe just a plot of
land and a couple of cows.

Then one day as we were driving back past
Greytown, KwaZulu-Natal, we came across a farm that
had fallen on hard times. The owner was dividing up
the land and was willing to sell us a portion of it. It
wasn't much of a bargain: the land had been neglected, it was overgrown with scrub wattle and there
was no water in sight, but I put down my deposit anyway. On 9 August 1977 we drove onto the farm for the
first time. "Welcome to your new home," I told the
children. We had no idea that this was to be the birth-
place of a ministry that would touch thousands by
God's grace. At the time it didn't even have a name.

"Where shall we build the house?" I asked Jill.

She pointed. "Over there looks like a good place."

I went and paced out the ground. "OK," I said. "This
will be home."

Meanwhile, we needed a roof over our heads, so I
hired a caravan for R200 and parked it among the
bushes. Jill was an angel: she never complained, even
though she had three children to look after and was
six months pregnant. Every day she took a plastic
bucket in the car and drove to a neighbouring farm
for water, then came back and washed the children,
cooked their breakfast and got them ready for school.
Eventually the farmer took pity on us, and lent us his

2,000-litre water-cart, which we parked next to the caravan. Jill said it felt like luxury!

I employed the first couple of Zulu men who walked past, and they helped me build a traditional Zulu house. We cut down trees and cleared the ground, dug holes and put in corner posts. Then we cut saplings and nailed them to the uprights. The Zulu women made our bricks, trampling the mud to make it sticky and cutting it into blocks. We stacked the bricks inside the saplings, and when they were dry we coated the outside in another layer of mud, covered it in cement and painted it with whitewash. I wanted a thatched roof but that takes time – and money – so we put on a tin roof. We finished it in three weeks and moved in. It wasn't much bigger than the caravan, but it felt like a palace to us. Later we knocked a hole in the wall and built more rooms, but we never replaced it – we still live in the same house.

I was starting from square one – I didn't speak Zulu, I didn't know the land, I didn't even know when the rains would come in this new country. All I had was my physical strength, my farming skills, and my determination to build a new life for our little family. At that time we were regarded with some disdain by the local farmers, as if we were gypsies or tinkers: we had come from nowhere; we were camping in primitive conditions with no telephone, no water, no lights, no radio, nothing. Even the local Zulu people laughed at us.

"These white people are living harder than us," they said. "Give them six months and they'll be gone!"

One of our first needs was water. I had turned

down the offer of a water diviner, but managed to find a damp spot by myself. We dug down with a spade and found a spring, so we could pump water for the house and give back the water-cart. I was determined to be self-sufficient. By the time Fergus was born in November we were settled in our new home.

The farm is about fifteen kilometres from Greytown in KwaZulu-Natal, close to the border with Lesotho and the beautiful Drakensberg Mountains. The climate is temperate, and we have four seasons like the UK: in the winter the frost is so thick it looks like snow. We are around 1,000 metres above sea level and grow potatoes, beans, mealies (maize) and fruit – apples, plums and pears.

In those early days, though, there was a huge amount of work to do. The land had been neglected and was overgrown with wattle, a vicious invader plant that quickly populates good arable land and has to be pulled out by the roots. It was a tremendously hard job, and the main reason why we were able to buy the land so cheaply.

I worked seven days a week from morning to night, carving that little farm out of the bush with one tractor. It was a lonely time. I was a stranger in a strange land. Our nearest neighbours were two or three kilometres away, mostly white farmers who spoke English or Afrikaans. The local population was Zulu, and although in those days I couldn't speak the language, I managed to hire half a dozen men to help me build the house, shed and workshop, and help clear the land. I installed a lighting plant, put in the telephone, piped the water. I was working an 18-hour day and some of the Zulus left without collecting their wages because they couldn't keep up with the pace I set.

"This *malungu* (white man) is *hlanya* (crazy)," they said.

I managed to secure a contract to grow seed mealies and the first year we got a bumper crop. It was a tremendous achievement: growing the crop commercially for seed (rather than for food) is very demanding. It has to be hand-reaped and requires lots of manual labour. That year I employed between 80 and 100 workers on the farm: some of them worked for cash, and others in exchange for food, building materials or fuel.

"I'll pay off the balance on the farm in one year," I promised the farmer who sold it to me. That was quite a statement. Some farmers take a couple of generations to pay off the mortgage on their farm, but I wanted to prove myself. I kept telling myself that once the farm was secured, I would find the peace and contentment I longed for, but the harder I worked, the more I wondered what I was doing it all for. I was experiencing the truth of Mark 8:36: "What good is it for a man to gain the whole world, yet forfeit his soul?"

Deep down I knew I needed God in my life, but just then I didn't have time to stop and think about what was happening to me. There was one small sign that God had us in his hand. One day we had a telephone call from Pretoria, the headquarters of the Ministry of Agriculture. The land surveyor told me he had officially subdivided the farm, and our section of it had to be registered with its own name.

I asked him to hang on for a moment and called to Jill.

"The man wants us to name the farm," I told her. "Can you think what to call it?"

Jill thought for a moment. "*Shalom*'s a good name," she said. "It means 'Peace'." So Shalom became its name.

Of course, peace was just what I didn't have. The unremitting stress and hard work were taking their toll and I was on a very short fuse.

One night an eight-tonne lorry drove onto my land. I went over and spoke to the big Zulu driver.

"What are you doing here?" I asked. "What do you want?"

"Oh, I've come to collect my timber," he replied.

I was furious. When I bought the farm nothing was said about timber belonging to anyone else.

"This is my farm now. Get off my land."

The Zulu glared at me. "The last farmer sold it to me. I've come for my timber and I'm going to get it."

What I said to him is unprintable. "If you go into my land and get stuck, you're in big trouble," I warned him. "Get off my farm right now."

For answer he put his foot on the accelerator and drove off into the plantation. It was 10 p.m. before I heard the vehicle coming out again.

"I know what's happened," I muttered to Jill. "He's got stuck in there and he's had to call another 20 Zulus to pull him out. That's cost him money and he's coming to settle with me."

I rushed outside with a flashlight, swearing as I went.

"What do you think you're doing?" I shouted.

He put his lorry in gear and drove it straight at me. I had to leap out of the way, and I shook my fist at him as he drove off into the night.

Two hours later I heard another vehicle – a kombi (truck) this time. I put two and two together and made five.

"They've come back for us, Jill. Stay in the house with the children!"

I grabbed an axe and went outside. A group of young men were climbing out of the truck, so I held up my weapon as I went towards them. I would get them before they got me! I'll never forget the look on their faces as they jumped back in their vehicle and took off down the road. One of the workmen told me later that they were the sons of the old man driving the lorry. He hadn't come home and they were out looking for him.

It was an eventful night by any standards, but the most worrying thing was my state of mind: quick to anger, suspicious of everyone, and ready to be violent. I had achieved so much on the farm, but emotionally I was close to breaking point.

3
A New Beginning

*T*ime went by and we began to feel that the Greytown area was our home. The older children were settled in school, we had established ourselves as successful farmers – that bumper crop had enabled us to pay off all our debts – and we had become accepted in the district. I made time for a few games of polocrosse, sometimes called "poor man's polo" because you use only one horse instead of the usual four needed for polo. It's a very fast, tough game – a bit like rugby on horseback – and right up my alley. I loved the rough and tumble, and made friends among the other players.

The farm was doing well, and the family was thriving. My lovely wife had made a real home out of the quaint and rustic Zulu house we had built. Jill studied fine art at university, and has an eye for beauty, and the gift of making the house a warm, welcoming and relaxing place to be. What more could a man want?

All the same, I wasn't satisfied. My biggest dream had been to own my own farm, and now I had succeeded, but at what cost? Having the title deeds in my name had made no difference to me at all. The emptiness inside me increased. I'd go off to the country club every Friday evening and down a couple of beers, thinking that perhaps they would fill the gap. Sometimes I had more than a couple, but the emptiness remained.

One day I had to drive some Zulu labourers back to their homeland in the truck, so I left my *induna* (foreman), Simeon Bengu, in charge of the farm.

"Simeon," I told him, "I'll be back about sunset. Look after the farm and take care of the tractor."

That evening as I drove in at the gate I saw two men standing under a tree. One was Simeon and the other Isaiah Mthwethwa, the tractor driver. I knew at once that something was wrong.

"All right," I said. "Now what?"

"Big problem!"

"What problem? A puncture? Have you run out of diesel?"

The *induna* shifted uncomfortably from foot to foot. "Big accident."

"Show me."

We walked up a bush track to a field we were busy ploughing, and as we turned the corner my knees nearly buckled. There, lying on its back, with its front axle completely ripped off, was my large green tractor – my pride and joy, and my only means of creating a farm in this dense bushveldt.

Isaiah had allowed Simeon to drive the tractor – something I had expressly forbidden – and he had taken a corner too fast and hit a tree stump. I looked at the tractor in despair. The exhaust pipe and manifold were completely crushed, the battery was hanging upside down, and oil and diesel were everywhere. I stood in silence for a moment and then turned on them. The men took one look at my face and fled into the mealies.

"Come back!" I shouted. "It's OK. Let's see what we can do."

They came out gingerly, but immediately my blood began to boil again. I didn't need this kind of aggravation. Why couldn't they do as they were told? How could I get on with the farm work without my tractor? I took another look at the twisted hunk of metal and lost control: I swung out with my fist and both men ran for their lives.

Once I had cooled down and managed to get control of myself, I went in search of the two men.

"You'll have to help me tonight after work. There's nothing else we can do. We'll have to fix this tractor ourselves because I don't have the money to call a mechanic."

They agreed. It took hours of hard work into the early hours of the morning before we could get the tractor running again. Without it, I couldn't plough or disc my fields, and planting time was running short.

That night I couldn't sleep. My heart was racing, my mouth was dry and the same angry thoughts kept racing round in my head. I felt as if I was driving a car down the highway with my foot jammed on the accelerator – the engine was screaming, but I couldn't switch it off. I felt totally out of control and I was horrified. I thought I was having a heart attack.

I was a proud man who had been brought up in the old school – cowboys don't cry – but I knew I needed help. Luckily Paddy Reynolds, our family doctor, was a polocrosse friend, so I went and talked to him. I explained how hard I had been working, how hard I found it to switch off, and about my uncontrollable outbursts of anger.

"Angus," he said, "take these pills. They'll sort you out and quieten you down a bit."

"Are these tranquillisers?"

"Yes. Just take them, will you?"

I was shattered. If I needed tranquillisers, I knew things must be getting out of hand. Reluctantly I took one when I got home, but it didn't have any effect. I was still wide awake all night. I felt keyed up and exhausted at the same time, and I didn't know where else to turn. I felt broken.

Things went on in this way for a while. One day I was walking in the fields with Robyn. She was only about three years old, and she held on to my little finger as we checked the corn. I looked down at her happy little face and thought, "I don't know how I'm going to cope. I don't know how I'm going to take care of this little girl. I don't know what's going to happen to this child if I crack up."

No one but Paddy and Jill knew how bad I was feeling; Jill was torn to see the state I was in, but she was powerless to help me. Fortunately, God intervened before I had a complete breakdown.

The local Methodist church was running a lay witness mission, and someone invited us along. At that time I hadn't been near a church for a long time: I used to say that the local country club was my church, because I went there every week. We didn't particularly want to go to this mission meeting, but it was difficult to refuse, so we went along on the Saturday night. It was a strange experience. When we arrived people were singing along with a music group; some were clapping, and others had their hands raised in the air. It was all very different from the stolid Presbyterian services of my youth. I looked longingly at the door, but the way out was blocked by an elderly couple who had come in and were sitting next to us. They introduced themselves as Frank and Myra Hambidge.

"Why don't you come along to church tomorrow morning?" asked Frank. "This group will be taking the service."

I didn't really want to spend Sunday morning in church, but I was touched by the invitation. These people seemed to be genuinely interested and caring, and they looked so happy. I could do with some of that.

"OK," I said, "we'll be there."

We got up early the next morning to get ready for church, but we had four children to deal with. By the time we had the whole family ready we were running late, and when we arrived the church was full. The Lord has a real sense of humour: we trooped in and had to walk right up to the front to find seats. Everyone in the congregation knew that Angus Buchan and his family were in church that morning.

"Morning, farmer!" smiled Frank Hambidge, and I smiled back. At least I knew somebody.

There was an air of expectancy in the church. The lay people were sharing their testimonies, and I sat there with my mouth open as I listened to them. For the first time in my life I saw strong men cry as they told how the Lord had taken care of their needs, restored their businesses and done wonderful things in their lives.

One guy was a building contractor. He started weeping as he told how his business had gone down and he had contemplated suicide. Then he found Jesus, and now he had a reason to live. Another man told how his marriage had been breaking up, when the Lord had brought him and his wife together again. Their stories pierced my heart. For years I had had no interest in religion, but these men's words had the ring of truth. I wanted to be part of this kind of life; I wanted to know more.

"What about you? Would you like to accept Jesus Christ as your Lord and Saviour today?" I looked at the speaker and realised that was exactly what I wanted to do. Jill and I walked to the front of the church with many others, and knelt before the Lord. We prayed the sinner's prayer together, saying sorry for our sins and asking Jesus to rule our hearts, and a miracle happened. Jesus came into our lives.

I knew it was true, though there were no bells ringing, no bright lights, no drama – just a deep assurance in my soul.

In fact it was only later, as I was walking in the maize fields, that I really understood what had happened. I knew that from now on, Jesus Christ was in total control of my life. No matter what happened, my Lord would take care of everything. Jesus was mine and I was his – for ever. An amazing peace came over me, and all my emotional torment, the fear and anxiety and stress fell away. From that moment I called those fields my "green cathedral", the place where I love to walk and talk with my Lord.

That afternoon a couple from the church came to visit us. Eustace and Trish van Rooyen were believers, and they had something special to say.

"We saw you respond to the altar call in church. Did you mean it?"

I did, with all my heart, and so did Jill. We told them so.

"Then I have a challenge for you," said Eustace. "If you mean business with Jesus, then tell the first three people you meet tomorrow morning what has happened to you."

It was some challenge. On Friday night I had been in the pub with the boys, and on Sunday morning I had given my life to Christ. My friends were mostly rough characters like me, and they would be pretty surprised by all this. I wondered if I could do it.

The first person I met the next morning was a local dairy farmer. He was a really tough character – the regimental sergeant major of the local army camp for reservists. We were on our way to buy cattle at a neighbouring farm, and as I drove I felt the Holy Spirit prompting me to speak.

"Ian," I said, "I've got something to tell you."

"Well?"

I was silent for a moment. In my head I was praying, "What do I say?"

The answer came clearly: "Just tell him!"

"I've become a Christian. I've accepted Jesus Christ as my Lord and Saviour."

There was a pause, but he didn't laugh. He just looked at me and said, "I'm pleased for you, Angus."

That gave me courage. "What about you?" I said. "Have you ever thought about it?"

"No, that's not for me," he replied, and we said no more about it that day. Ian was the first person I ever witnessed to, and my words took a long time to sink in. Two years later he gave his life to Christ.

At the time, however, I was just relieved that I'd told someone. It wasn't so bad. Who was next? The fertiliser rep came to the farm, so I told him. After that, I told everybody I saw – I couldn't keep quiet! I'm still telling everybody about Jesus. My friends were convinced because they could see the change in me. For one thing, I used to have the filthiest mouth in town, but when I became a Christian the habit of swearing left me completely. The Lord delivered me from that immediately.

Jill and I were excited by our faith. Our lives were transformed, and it was an extra blessing that we had come to Jesus together. We shared everything we learned, reading Christian books, listening to tapes and music and reading the Bible.

All farmers get up early in the morning, but I began to get up extra early. Jill and I had tea together and then I went into my little office to have a quiet time with the Lord. This time with Jesus became the most important part of my day, as he spoke to me through prayer, the scriptures and devotional readings. It was a discipline the Lord was building into my life that became a lifeline to me. Sometimes I would go out into the fields to pray: the maize fields are very special to me. In the rainy season in summer, when the plants are tallest, the long green leafy stalks almost touch each other at the top. In the autumn the entire crop turns a beautiful golden colour. I love to stand there and thank God for blessing us so richly with his amazing creation.

We worshipped every week at the little Methodist church in Greytown, and we soon got involved in every Christian activity there. The minister, Errol Hind, was a wonderful encouragement to us, and a great teacher through his example and God's word.

Three months after giving my life to the Lord I began preaching. It was very exciting. I would study the Bible and pray, and miraculously find that I had the words to say. I wanted to tell everyone what Jesus had done for me. The local church council wanted me to take an exam to become a local preacher, but somehow there was never time, so they called me an "exhorter" and let me go on preaching anyway.

Jill and I wanted everything God had for us, so when we read about some special services in town, we went along. There we began to experience God in a new way, and we were filled with the Holy Spirit; shortly afterwards we were both baptised with water. It was the start of a whole new dimension of our walk with Christ.

God was beginning to use us and we loved it. One weekend I was playing polocrosse with one of my old boozing buddies, Jan. He kept looking at me sideways and eventually said, "What's happened to you, Angus? You seem different."

What an opportunity! The words poured out as I

told him about finding Jesus and his incredible peace. Jan was interested. "Can I come and see you? I'd like to know more about this."

I rushed home to Jill. "Jan's coming round after work tomorrow. He wants to know the Lord!"

We were excited, until the reality of it hit us. How did you lead someone to Jesus? What should we say to him? Should we call in the minister? "Lord," we prayed, "show us what to do."

Then I remembered a little booklet about faith that I had been given by Campus Crusade. I would share that with him. The next afternoon Jan arrived at the farm, and we went out into the maize fields together.

"Are you sure you want to receive the Lord Jesus Christ as your Saviour?" I asked.

"Yes!" he replied, so we prayed together. It was a wonderful moment. We were both so happy and filled with the Holy Spirit that we were laughing and crying for joy at the same time.

My mum was another person who saw the change in us. She and Dad had moved to Greytown to be near the family, and Jill and I regularly called in for a cup of tea. One day we were sitting in her kitchen round the big wood stove when she started to cry.

"It isn't the same any more," she said. "You and Jill are different. You've grown away from me and I can't stand it."

She was afraid that she had lost us, though I told her we loved her more than ever before.

"Mum," I said, "Jill and I are different because we've accepted Jesus. You can do it too. Would you like to?"

"Yes, I would," she said, and she prayed the sinner's prayer with us in her soft Scottish accent. We all cried tears of joy that day, except Dad. He still wasn't having any of it. Mum read her Bible eagerly, and when I called in to see her she would amaze me with her insight into the scriptures. When I became a lay preacher she would come and sit in the front row with her white head slightly bowed as she listened. I would look down from the pulpit and it gave me such joy to see her there.

I felt that talking to people about Jesus was a great privilege. Andy was a young gold-miner from the Transvaal who came to spend some time with us at Shalom; his marriage was in trouble and he was trying to find some answers. Every morning he would walk down to the fields around 7.30 and jump onto the tractor. We had already been out there for three hours, so I was ready take a break. We would talk about his problems as the day grew brighter and the early-morning freshness was still in the air.

One particular morning Andy sat in silence, gazing at the beauty all around him. We watched the Zulu labourers checking the planter and making sure that the seed was falling out properly into the prepared soil, and I prayed for this big strong miner who needed the Lord so much.

"Lord, prepare his heart and let the seed of your word take root there."

I talked to him about Jesus and his brokenness touched my heart. I saw tears glistening in his eyes as the Holy Spirit showed him his sin and he acknowledged the ways in which he had been at fault. Andy came to repentance and started thanking the Lord for the goodness of his grace. I could see that Jesus was healing him of all the hurts he had experienced. As the tractors moved through the fields planting the crop of maize, so the Holy Spirit was moving in his heart and planting spiritual seed there.

Andy works as a cage operator, taking men up and down some of the deepest mine shafts in the world. Down there in the darkness, he told me, whenever he feels depressed he turns his mind to the memory of Shalom, the green maize fields, the cattle, and our early morning walks as we talked together about Jesus.

There's nothing I love more than leading someone to my Lord. I marvel at the way he uses the smallest details of our lives as a witness to his saving grace.

One day I decided we needed a windmill on the farm, so I called Angus Flockhart at Stewarts and Lloyds. He came to the farm and advised me about the size and type of windmill I needed, and promised to make sure it was installed correctly.

"Now, Angus," he said as he was leaving, "the company logo usually goes on the tail of the windmill. Shall we put Shalom's name up there?"

"No," I smiled, "I want a fish painted on the tail-piece."

"A fish?" He looked at me as if I was insane. "Why on earth would you want a fish?"

"It was a sign used by the early Christians," I told him. "That way, we have a sign of who we are right up there for everyone to see."

"Well, if that's what you want, OK."

A few months later he was at home watching TV, drinking a beer and feeling very low. His wife had died of cancer only three months before, leaving him with two small children to care for. Something on the TV screen caught his attention – a windmill with a fish on the tail! If it had been a name he would hardly have given it a second glance.

"I know that windmill!" he exclaimed, and turned up the sound. It was a programme about local farmers and how Jesus had made a difference in their lives. Jill and I were interviewed, and we were able to say how we had come to know the Lord and what he had done for us.

When the programme came to an end, Angus Flockhart telephoned Jill.

"I want to come and see you both. I must talk to you," he said.

He came the very next Saturday, and our children played together while I took him for a ride round the farm. He was a tough Scotsman like me, but by now I had learned that no one is too tough for the Lord. We talked all afternoon until the sun began to set behind the pine trees.

"Do you want Jesus to come into your life?" I asked him.

He took off his tam o'shanter and bowed his head. Standing there in the golden fields in the sunset, with the tears running down his face, he asked Jesus to be his Lord and Saviour. He gave the Lord his life, and Jesus has kept his promises to him. His life has been totally transformed; he is married to a wonderful Christian, they have three beautiful children and the

Lord is blessing them. Our Lord is so faithful. I never fail to be amazed at the beauty and simplicity of the gospel.

4
Farming for Jesus

I became a Christian in 1979, and my life immediately began to change. I was still a farmer – I will always be a farmer – but now I had a new priority. My aim was first and foremost to live my life for Christ, and to do his will. I was just beginning to discover what a privilege and pleasure it is to serve the living God. I was so thankful that he had saved me, and that he was now in control of all the details of my redeemed life. I was about to discover what that meant.

Every year we burn firebreaks on the farm: after the first frosts the grass becomes tinder-dry, and it's easy for fire to break out. So once the rains have stopped, but before everything gets too dry, we go round the farm and burn off wide strips of land in a controlled way, with a water-cart following the burn to put out the fire. That way, if a fire should start in a field later, it can't spread because it will die out at the edge where there is nothing left to burn.

That autumn we set out to burn the firebreaks as usual on a bright windy day in April. Simeon Bengu, my *induna*, was waiting in the yard with a gang of farm workers, and he agreed that it would be a good day for the burn: the grass was still fairly green, so there was no risk of the fire getting out of control.

We started burning at around 9 a.m., and at first everything went as planned. Then, quite suddenly, the wind changed: all at once it was blowing a gale, and a loose clump of burning grass was lifted high in the air and blown across the road into a forest that hadn't been touched for years. The dry undergrowth caught fire immediately. We watched in horror as the flames spread rapidly, fanned by the strong wind.

"We've got to put it out!" I shouted. There was a note of panic in my voice. Our farm is bordered by two big timber companies, H. L. & L. and the Lion Match Company. Both have hundreds of acres of timber, and I shuddered to think of what might happen if the fire spread from our farm into their forests.

I ran to my bakkie – a small open-backed farm truck – and took off down the road, driving so fast that the tailgate flew off. I screeched to a halt outside the house.

"Jill!" I yelled. "We've got a fire! Get on the phone to the other farmers and ask them to help us, right now. It's bad."

Small farmers have limited fire-fighting equipment, and turn out to help each other in these emergencies. I knew we couldn't handle that fire by ourselves: the situation was desperate.

I rushed back to the fire and saw that it had already spread to the pine trees and become a raging inferno: the pine resin began to explode. I had taken off my shirt earlier that morning as I worked in the heat; as

I ran past, one of the trees exploded and all the hair on the back of my neck and down my back was burned off. I didn't even notice in the frantic rush to try to beat out the flames in the undergrowth.

Within half an hour all our neighbours had arrived with their fire-fighting equipment: water-tankers, tractors with high-pressure hoses and water-carts. We were going to need everything we could get to help us as we tried to contain the fire. The heat was incredible.

Our neighbours couldn't stay to help us for long: the next day was Good Friday and they had to return to their farms to pay their labourers before the holiday. As I watched them leave, I realised with a hollow feeling in the pit of my stomach that we couldn't do this alone. The fire was going to jump the fence.

Just then a scripture flashed into my mind: "Whatever you ask for in prayer, believe that you have received it and it will be yours" (Mark 11:24). I turned to the Zulu driver beside me, who was busy directing a hose onto the fire.

"I'm going to pray and ask the Lord Jesus Christ to please send rain," I said.

He looked at me in surprise and began to laugh. "There will be no rain! The rainy season is over! Can't you see that there are no clouds in the sky?"

It was true: the sky was clear, the wind was blowing and there wasn't the slightest sign of rain. All the same, I closed my eyes and said a simple prayer.

Less than five minutes later we heard a mighty clap of thunder! The driver and I turned round in astonishment. I was trembling all over, and the Zulu's mouth was open and his eyes were like saucers. The impossible had happened. The wind had changed direction and dark clouds were rolling in from the south. A few minutes later a gentle drizzle began to fall over Shalom, and I watched in awe as the rain doused the raging fire. God's goodness overwhelmed me.

The wind dropped, and it rained all afternoon and overnight. The next day, while Jill took the children into town to the Good Friday service, I patrolled the perimeter of the burned area, armed with a 300-litre sprayer. I didn't need it: the rain had completely extinguished the fire. I sat on my tractor and prayed. "Lord, you're so good," I said. "Thank you for saving us."

Events like this really built my faith. I learned that God cares about the detail of our lives, and is power-ful to help us. My foreman Simeon rejoiced with me at this miracle. He had become a Christian not long before, and he is now a treasured brother in Christ. This raw Zulu man is illiterate, but he is the salt of the earth. He is strong, with huge hands like baseball mitts, and he has worked side by side with me for years, as we carved out this farm together from an expanse of wild overgrown land. Simeon has become my best friend, not just my farm foreman.

When Simeon lost his son Musa, he asked me to conduct the funeral service, and I was deeply moved. My boys have become his boys, because now he has only one son, and in the Zulu tradition it's a very bad thing not to have many children. I would trust that man with my life, as he would me; I would do any-thing for him. He loves the Lord, and if I am going away on a long campaign he will come and pray with me before I leave, in his native Zulu language. He puts his massive mitt heavily on top of my head, and I know that I am truly blessed.

At this time I was taking every opportunity to tell people about Jesus, including my farm workers. Growing seed corn requires a lot of hand work, hoeing the weeds and de-tasselling the maize, so we always brought in a lot of female labourers during the rainy season. We have a contact lady who goes into the Zulu homeland where the people live in clans or tribes, and she recruits our workers, bringing them back on a lorry. These ladies then stay on the farm for the season, living in a big Zulu hut which sleeps 80 or so.

I always prayed that the Lord would speak to these women and save their souls, and I used to talk to them as best I could in my very poor Zulu.

"Jesus Christ is our Saviour," I told them. "You must serve him, and not your idols and ancestral spirits. They have no power, but God can protect you." I believed what I said to them, but I didn't expect my faith in God's power to be tested.

One day in late November there was a tremendous thunderstorm. Lightning flashed across the sky, and rain was drumming on our roof so loudly that we could hardly hear ourselves speak. Suddenly I heard the sound of women screaming outside.

"*Khosani, Khosani*, please come! Something terrible has happened!"

I went to the window. I could see a group of black women huddled against the fence with blankets wrapped around them.

"What's wrong?" I shouted, but I couldn't hear their reply. I went out to talk to them. They were all shouting and talking at once, but eventually I understood that lightning had struck the hut where the women slept. Fifty of them had been struck to the ground, and they had all recovered except one. They had left this woman lying in the hut covered by a blanket.

"She is dead," they said. "You must come now."

I jumped into the bakkie with some of the women and drove over to the hut, about 500 metres away. It was a traditional Zulu building, very big but with a small entrance, so low that you have to get down on your hands and knees to go in.

"Bring her outside," I said. They refused. They wouldn't help lift her into the bakkie so that we could take her to the hospital – they wouldn't even touch her.

"You told us your God was powerful," they said. "You pray and ask him to touch this woman. Then we'll see if this Jesus you talk about is real."

I was stunned. What could I do? I cried out to the Lord: "You have to help me now. I don't know what to do."

I crawled inside. A fire was burning in the middle of the hut and the interior was dark and smoky, so at first I couldn't see much. Outside, the women began wailing and lamenting. One of the women still inside the hut pointed to the body, lying by the wall. I went over. I had no idea whether the woman was dead or unconscious, but I acted in raw faith, in fear and trembling. I laid my hands on her, closed my eyes and prayed.

"Lord, please bring healing to this woman's body."
I felt a strong impression from the Holy Spirit that I
should lift the woman up, so I bent over her, lifted her
to her feet and let her go. She remained standing. The
wailing outside had stopped, and there was deathly
silence.

"Can you hear me?" I asked.

She nodded.

"Lift up your hands to God."

She lifted her arms into the air and pandemonium
broke out: the women inside the hut were screaming
and shouting, dancing and singing, and the women
outside heard their cries and joined in, singing
praises to God. It was a wonderful, awesome moment.

The farm labourers spoke of nothing else for
weeks. God had performed a miracle before their eyes,
and they told everyone they knew.

It was a lesson for me to trust in God, but we forget
so easily. The next time we had a problem, I didn't
turn to God first – but the family did. The problem
was our beautiful Jersey cow, Hester. We were having
breakfast in the kitchen one morning when I happened to glance outside and saw that the cow was
lying on her side.

I ran out to look at her, and saw at once that she
was very sick. I hurried back to the phone and called
the vet in Greytown.

"Rob, come quick," I said. "Our cow's dying. We
only have one, and we need her."

"What are the symptoms?" he said.

I was busy telling him about her shallow breathing
and her glazed eyes when I noticed that Jill and the

children had left the table. I looked out of the window and there they were – Jill in her dressing gown, Andrew, Lindi and Robyn, and even little Fergus who was just a toddler – marching across the paddock. They knelt around the sick cow, laid their hands on her and bowed their heads. I knew they were praying. Then they all stood up – and so did the cow. Hester began grazing as if nothing had happened.

"Hello?" said the vet. "Are you still there, Angus?"

I was deeply embarrassed. "Er – don't worry. You don't need to come out. Everything's OK."

"What do you mean?" asked Rob. "What's going on?"

I had to tell him the truth.

"Jill and the children just laid their hands on the cow and prayed for her. The Lord has healed my cow."

There was silence at the other end of the line. I said goodbye quickly and put the phone down. Then I bowed my head and apologised to the Lord for my lack of faith. I was learning.

In those early days, as our faith grew, so did our involvement with the work of the local church. We began to take an interest in working with young people: there wasn't a great deal for them to do in Greytown, and we had all this land. We opened the farm to the youngsters, and built a huge obstacle course in the forest for them to play on, with rope walks, tunnels and ladders. They loved it. We built two authentic Zulu huts with a cold shower and a latrine, and the kids would come and camp there. It gave us a wonderful opportunity to get to know them and share our faith with them.

We did that for two or three seasons, until there began to be more activities available for them in the town. Then the Lord led us on to new work. We kept coming across other people who had problems – who were underprivileged, homeless or lonely – and we took them into our home. We would counsel them and let them share in the life of the farm: it was a place of hard work, good food, a busy family life, a lot of love and laughter, and plenty of prayer. They thrived on it, and many of their emotional hurts began to be healed as they came to faith in Jesus Christ.

I truly believe that the people who came to us were sent by the Lord – either because we were able to help them, or because they had something to teach us. There's an old story about a new missionary doctor who flew in to a remote outpost in Africa. The older missionaries greeted him and said, "Have you come to Africa to help the poor black people?"

"Yes," he replied.

"Well, you're wrong," they answered. "God has sent you to Africa so the poor black people can teach you about yourself." That's what happened to me. God had so many lessons to teach me in those days. He used those people as sandpaper to scrub at my selfishness and my preconceived ideas about what I could do for him.

They say that new Christians should be locked up for the first six months, and I think that's true. We were so eager to work for the Lord that we made lots of mistakes: God must have sent his guardian angels to look after us, we were so naïve. We took in one young man of Afrikaans descent whose father had been a government minister. We let him sleep in the living room next to our children's rooms (at that time we had no doors, only partitions between the rooms), until we realised how deeply mentally disturbed he was. He would behave normally for a while, then become irrational. He was immensely tall, and would reach up and try to push the roof off our house. One time he followed me in his car and tried to shunt my truck off the road. God protected us, but we weren't able to help that young man, and eventually he had to be institutionalised.

I tried getting some of our visitors to work on the farm, but that failed miserably. Many of them were drinkers or had mental problems, and they just upset the staff. They tried to take over and my Zulu workers, quite rightly, resented it. So I gave that up.

As the farm prospered we had been able to buy up some adjoining farmland so we had plenty of space, and after a while, we started building a few small cottages to house our visitors. Some of them stayed with us for a long while. Glenn came to us as a teenager from a broken home; he wrote his matriculation exam from the farm. He was a small lad to start with, but he blossomed while he was with us. He got interested in weight training, as I had been, and as he put on muscle he grew in confidence. When he went into the army (as all young white men in South Africa had to in those days) he became one of the elite Parabat fighting force. He came back to the farm to work and gave his life to Christ, and later I had the joy of conducting the service when he married his wife Tammy, who also came to work at Shalom. They now live in the

USA. I have been blessed with so many spiritual children, and I thank the Lord for them – young men whom I've had the privilege of leading to the Lord, and nurtured and supported physically, emotionally and spiritually. There are too few spiritual fathers around these days, and there is a great need for men who are able to fill this role.

We once had a strange encounter with a group of three Sabras (that is, Jews who were born in the land of Israel – these were the next generation of families who had come from the Warsaw ghetto). The two men had been deceived into coming to South Africa to work, by a man who had given them nothing he promised – no food, work or accommodation. One had brought his wife and little son, and they were now completely destitute. I managed to get them work locally until they saved enough money for their fare back to Israel, and let them use a cottage next to our house.

They were not religious Jews, but one night they had a tremendous encounter with God. They had invited me into their house to share their Shabbat meal, and when I prayed they began to weep. Hananya, the eldest man, took the *yarmulka* from his head and gave it to me. "I make a vow in the presence of God over the life of my son," he said. "When you come to Israel we will look after you as you have cared for us." From our point of view, we were just using what we had to work for the Lord. James says, "Do not merely listen to the word, and so deceive yourselves. Do what it says" (James 1:22).

God is no respecter of persons: he uses housewives,

children, farmers, and anyone who is willing to believe in him. The Christian life is a life of faith. "We live by faith, not by sight" (2 Corinthians 5:7). I was trying to explain that to a man from the city one day. Pete was an alcoholic who had come to stay at the farm, and I was trying to impress on him that we have to trust God no matter what our circumstances.

"Pete," I said, "it doesn't matter about the past and what has happened in your life. What is important is your personal walk with God. Romans 8:28 says, 'We know that in all things God works for the good of those who love him.' If you put Jesus Christ first in your life, he will take care of the rest."

"That's all very well for you, Angus," said Pete despondently. "You have a wife who loves you, beautiful children, and you're doing the thing you love best – farming. I've got nothing. My wife left me, my children don't want to know me, I don't have a friend in the world and I don't have a penny to my name."

I glanced out of the window. The fields were a wonderful green and the corn was already head-high: it was going to be a fine crop.

"Lord," I prayed silently, "how can I convince him? How can I show him that as long as we put you first, you'll sort everything out?"

Right then a dark cloud came over the farm and the wind began to howl. Within a few minutes we were at the centre of a ferocious storm – the hailstones made a tremendous drumming noise on the roof. After fifteen minutes it had all blown over: the wind dropped, the rain and hail stopped and the sun came out. Pete looked shocked. He had been a farmer and he knew what this meant: a hailstorm like that could decimate the crop, and the only thing we were growing that year was seed maize. Crop failure meant immediate bankruptcy.

We went outside. The magnificent maize that had been standing so tall had been flattened. It looked as though someone had driven a tractor or a herd of cattle over it. We walked out through the fields and I could see Pete studying my face as he waited for my reaction. I had just been telling him that Jesus Christ is in control of our lives and that we should praise him in all circumstances. Now I had to do exactly that.

"Pete," I said, "nothing changes. Jesus Christ is still Lord. I've given my life to him, along with the farm and the family. I choose to trust and praise him, whatever happens."

To be honest, praise was the last thing I felt like, but I gritted my teeth and thanked God, as we walked the whole hundred hectares of maize. It was all gone.

That night the devil had a good time. I couldn't sleep. "Maybe the bank will be kind to you," he said. "Maybe they'll let you keep the farm till the end of the season. You're finished."

I shut my eyes tight in the darkness. "I believe in Jesus Christ," I said. "With God all things are possible."

Three days later an amazing sight met our eyes. That entire maize crop picked itself up off the ground and stood once more. It had a permanent bend in the stalk, but it was standing, and at the end of the season we had our bumper crop of seed mealies. All praise and honour to God! Jesus Christ is Lord indeed.

That's not the end of the story. A few years later I

was sitting in church in Greytown listening to the preacher talk about faith. Pete had left us long ago and gone back on the road, and I had no idea he was in church until I heard his voice booming out from the back pews.

"If you want to know about faith, I can tell you," he said. And he told everyone the story of how the maize had been flattened by the storm and risen again, when we had continued to praise God. I'm still praying for Pete, that he will come to trust the God of miracles, and that the Lord will work miracles in his life.

For the first ten years after I gave my life to the Lord, we continued in this way. Our children, Andrew, Lindi, Robyn, Fergus and little Jilly, were growing up and the farm was doing well. We went on farming for Jesus – bringing in a good harvest of crops year after year, and also doing his work among the poor and needy people he sent our way. Two things confirmed us in our assurance that this was God's will for us.

Soon after I made that decision for Christ, the Lord said to me, "First build a house of prayer." So in 1982 my father and I worked together to build a small chapel on the highest point of the farm. It has a thatched roof and is big enough to seat up to 150 people, and there is a big picture window looking out over the whole farm – the forests, the paddocks with the grazing cattle, the maize lands and the windmill. Seeing that little chapel become the focus of prayer for the growing community at Shalom has been a wonderful thing. We hold services each Sunday in English and Zulu, white and black sitting together, men and women, old and young, and every church and denomination – all worshipping together because we love the Lord.

The other confirmation came one winter morning, when we held a baptism service on the farm. I had been approached by a group of Indians from another town, who asked if they could baptise some ladies. Our hearts were touched as we saw those dignified elderly Hindu ladies in their saris, breaking the ice at the edge of the pool and wading into the cold water up to their waists. Our pastor came out to perform the baptism, and afterwards he had a prophetic word for me and Jill. "This place is going to be like Noah's ark," he said. "It will be a refuge for those in the storms of life to come and receive peace and hope."

We prayed that it might be so. We never thought that the person most in need of those gifts might be me.

5
Auntie Angus

"Auntie Angus, where are you going?"

My nephew Alistair was four years old, and ever since he could talk he had called me "Auntie Angus". It was our joke.

"One of the tractors is stuck in a field, and I have to go and pull it out with another tractor."

Alistair loved tractors. Whenever I received a catalogue of John Deere tractors I would send it to him, so he could cut out the pictures and paste them on his bedroom walls. He loved visiting his "Auntie Angus" and the green tractors at Shalom; he followed me around like a shadow. Now his little hand reached up and took mine.

"Can I come too?"

The rest of the family was gathered on the lawn, celebrating Jill's birthday. My brother Fergus was there with his wife Joanne, and their other children, Fraser and the twins Kirstie and Sheena.

Fergus and I had always been close. At school we spent our break-times together, and on Saturdays we sat side by side at the cinema to watch the latest film. In the interval I was the one who handled the serious negotiations for swapping comics with the other kids: my little brother was too shy to leave his seat. When he left school Fergus made a name for himself as a professional golfer and moved away, but we stayed in touch: I had named my youngest son after him.

Now I looked down at Alistair's fair curly hair and his pleading blue eyes, so like his father's.

"You'll have to ask your dad, Alistair." I will always be grateful that I said that.

Alistair ran off and was soon back at my side, with Kirstie following him. Fergus was happy for them to go with me – I'd taken hundreds of children for tractor rides around the farm.

We walked out to the gate and I jumped into the tractor; Kirstie climbed in beside me and Alistair sat next to her. We set off.

It was a beautiful autumn afternoon: the mealies were beginning to turn golden and the farm looked lovely. At the thorn tree where the road curved round to the left I eased off the accelerator, so we were travelling very slowly. I have no idea exactly what happened next. All I know is that there was a sudden jolt and Alistair fell off the tractor. Before I could do anything, the rear wheel drove over the little boy. His small body was crushed.

I slammed on the brakes. Kirstie started screaming. "Take her home!" I called to one of the Zulu workers, as I ran to pick up Alistair. I gathered his limp body into my arms, and cried out to God for help.

By chance one of my neighbours had come to visit, and as he drove by he saw me standing there covered in blood, holding the little boy. He stopped his van and I climbed in beside him.

"Quick, Bob, take me to the house!"

I didn't even get out of the van as we screeched to a halt by the family party on the lawn. "Alistair's hurt! We're going to the hospital!"

I wept as Bob drove us at top speed into the town, crying to God to take control of the situation, though I could see how badly the child was hurt. Alistair died in my arms as we drove. My brother's youngest son breathed his last breath as I bent over him.

When we got to the hospital I scrambled out of the van and ran up the steps, shouting for help. The nurse took Alistair from my arms, placed him on a trolley and wheeled him into a side room. A doctor came and pronounced him dead.

Months afterwards, Fergus told me that as soon as he heard there had been an accident, he knew in his heart that Alistair was dead. Now he and Joanne came running down the long hospital corridor towards me.

"Angus ... my son?"

"I'm sorry, Fergie, I'm sorry. He's gone home to Jesus."

In that moment I realised how useless words could be. We stood there in the corridor with our arms wrapped around each other, weeping. Someone gave Fergus some forms to sign, and a few minutes later we were walking back down those steps. It was 3.30. Only an hour had passed since we had set off for our drive: an hour I will never forget. We were all stunned, but Fergus and Joanne found an incredible depth of grace in their hearts as we comforted each other. To this day they have never once blamed me for the accident, and the bond between us is as strong as ever.

When I got home I was in a state of shock. I stumbled into the bathroom to wash: there was blood on my hands and face. My clothes were soaked, and Jill had to take them away and burn them in the boiler. My daughter Lindi was crying as she threw her arms round my neck.

"Dad, don't blame yourself. It was an accident. It wasn't your fault!"

I was too distressed to think straight, but I wanted to be alone with God, so I went out into the maize fields. For the first time I realised how little possessions mean – even things as deeply loved and significant as my farm.

"Lord," I cried, "you can have the farm. You can have the mealies. You can have the tractors. I'll give up the shirt off my back, every cent I have – if you'll just give my brother his little son back again."

There was a stillness all around me as I walked, wrestling with God. Then I heard his voice speaking clearly to me in my heart.

"Angus, Alistair is mine and he is staying with me." I bowed my head and acknowledged the sovereignty of the Lord.

The news of Alistair's death – and the circumstances of it – spread rapidly through the district. We held a memorial service for little Alistair in the chapel at Shalom, and streams of cars came down the road to our home, from all around – believers and unbelievers, friends and acquaintances. The whole farming community gave us tremendous support and encouragement.

It was a terrible time: I was racked by guilt, and couldn't eat or sleep. The nights were the worst. Jill sat up with me night after night into the early hours of the morning, until she fell asleep out of sheer exhaustion, but every time I closed my eyes I felt the jolt of the tractor, heard Kirstie's screams, saw Alistair's little body lying limply in my arms.

The devil was quick to accuse me. The thoughts went round in my head day and night: "You killed your brother's son! It was your negligence that killed him. You should have been more careful. You're not worthy to be a witness for Jesus."

Greytown is a small, close-knit community, and the farmers in the area were among my good friends, but when I walked down the main street people would see me coming and duck into a shop rather than meet me. I knew it wasn't because they were condemning me – they simply didn't know what to say. Yet the thoughts would whisper in my heart: "See, even the town folk don't want anything to do with you. Your witness is over." I felt utterly isolated, cut off from normal life.

Friends would drive out to the farm to try to offer me some comfort, but end up breaking down and weeping themselves. Others would say, "How could God allow this responsibility to fall on you, when you're standing up so boldly for Jesus?" One Christian from a charismatic church challenged me: "Why didn't you raise him from the dead?" The devil echoed that one. "Yes, why didn't you? You don't have any faith."

My suffering was etched on my face. A good friend sought me out.

"Angus," he said, "do you have a gun?"

"Yes," I said, "I've got a shotgun I use for shooting vermin."

"Give it to me," he said. He was afraid I would kill myself.

In fact I had no intention of taking my own life. Although I was in the darkest place I had ever known, I knew the Lord was standing by my side.

As the battle raged on in my mind, I was reminded of a story I had heard about a Chinese convert. When the missionary asked him how he was coping with life as a Christian, he said, "It feels as if I have two dogs fighting within me, one white and one black."

"Which one is winning?" asked the missionary.

"It depends which one I feed," came the reply.

I knew that my strength came from the Lord alone, and I determined to spend more time with him than ever before. This battle would only be won on my knees.

Over the previous five years or so, ever since I became a Christian, I had made it a habit to spend time with Jesus in the early morning. During those dark days I would be awake long before the alarm went off at 4 a.m. Each morning before sunrise I would get up and go straight to my office. Every day I knelt before the Lord, and morning by morning he met me there in a very personal way. His word strengthened my heart and gave me courage. One morning Ephesians 6:10 gripped my spirit: "Be strong in the Lord and in his mighty power."

Whenever those terrible thoughts circled around me I clung on to the promises of God; the Lord stood by me and I was conscious of his presence. In the middle of the storm I would hear his voice: "My son, I am sovereign. Nothing can happen without my permission. I have taken Alistair home and he is happy and content. He does not want to come back."

I believed him. God is in total control of everything, and I determined never to ask "Why?" no matter how I felt. I recalled the story of Corrie and Betsy Ten Boom, imprisoned during the Second World War. As Corrie held her dying sister in her arms she cried out to God, "How can you let this happen?" Betsy looked up at her loving sister and said, "Corrie, if you know God you don't have to ask why."

I was so thankful for my faith, and I wondered how those who don't know the Lord can survive a trauma like this. It was only my relationship with Jesus Christ that kept me sane. I knew that I hadn't caused the accident to happen, and I knew that my all-seeing God did not blame me.

You never get used to living with something like this, but slowly I found myself getting stronger. God gave me peace as I waited on him in those early hours. It became the most precious time of my day.

Everyone has to face a time of testing. God never promised us a life free of trouble, only that he would walk with us through it. As I read the stories of great Christians, from Francis of Assisi to Billy Graham, from George Müller and William Carey to Hudson Taylor and John Wesley, I realised that every one of them without exception went through trials. Even the disciples – even our Master himself – passed through the fire.

I was devastated by the death of little Alistair. Seeing a child so innocent, so much loved, suffer and die presented a real challenge to my faith, and I was tormented by feelings of guilt. If I had not been a Christian I'm sure I would have ended up in an asylum, or as a drunk or a suicide. Even my dad, a man who had suffered through three and a half years of starvation in a prisoner-of-war camp, said to me, "Son, I have no idea what you went through."

The crux of the matter is, how did I get through the fire? I know how – through Jesus Christ never leaving me nor forsaking me. In those days I knew the presence of the Lord as never before. When the thoughts of the devil came into my head, saying that I was guilty of that child's death, that I had been irresponsible, I also heard the voice of the Holy Spirit, reminding me that nothing happens without God's permission. When the devil suggested that my witness was worthless because of my guilt, the Holy Spirit comforted me with the fact that Jesus Christ died for all sinners, and that I belonged to God. I had a choice: I could believe the lies of the devil, in which case I was on my way to suicide, or I could believe in the promises of God, and be taken through my time of trial.

Three months later Fergus woke up in the middle of the night. He telephoned me.

"Angus! The Lord has just given me such a clear vision of Alistair. I could see him – he was so happy and his face was glowing. I saw him running towards me through a field of grass, bright emerald green. I asked him if he wanted to come back to us, and he said, 'No, Dad, I'm waiting for you.' Angus, he gave me such peace. I wanted to share it with you. I know he's safe with Jesus."

I know that eternity is real. When I reach the pearly gates through the grace of God, there is going to be a little boy named Alistair waiting for me, and we will recognise each other. "Auntie Angus, welcome home!" I can almost hear his voice now. As I grew in Jesus through this experience, I came to realise that this life is nothing but a vapour, a puff of smoke that soon blows away. Our real eternal life is safe in the hands of God.

I rejoice that my whole family have found the Lord: Jill and I; my brother Fergus and his wife Joanne; all our children; my sister Morag; Jill's brother Ian, a Christian long before me, and his family; my mother, who came to Jesus after seeing the change in Jill and me. Even my trusted foreman, Simeon Bengu, had become a Christian. The only person who still held out against the Lord was my dad.

Dad had had a hard life: born in Scotland in 1917 in an area called Buchan, north of Aberdeen, he was the eldest of seven children. When he was twelve he won a scholarship to the Academy, but he wasn't able to take up his place. He had to go to work to help feed the family. He served an apprenticeship at the local smithy, where he fell in love with the blacksmith's daughter, Agnes.

He emigrated to South Africa and planned to go back to Scotland to marry, but the war intervened. He and Agnes had to wait six years before he was free to go home and marry her. They came back to Africa after the war, and Dad worked hard all his life to raise a family. He was a big man, and a hard one. "The man's not born that I'm afeard of," he would say. When I was a child he teased me about my churchgoing; when I came back to Christ in 1979 after my years in the wilderness he would still have nothing to do with religion. My faithful Jesus was working systematically in the lives of all my loved ones, but Dad would have none of it.

Shortly after my mother found the Lord we agreed that it would be a lot easier if Mum and Dad came to live at Shalom. Dad spent most of his time helping on the farm in any case, and Mum was lonely in the town because she couldn't drive any more. We bought a mobile home and set it up just behind the farmhouse, and they were very happy there.

A few years later Mum was called home to heaven, and Dad was devastated. He seemed to give up on life. Every evening I would go up to the little house and sit with him while he sipped a cold beer. We chatted about farming and sport, and I would try to get around to speaking about Jesus, but that made him really angry. I didn't think he would ever let me reach him with the gospel, but the family kept praying.

One day Dad was taken ill, and we took him to the hospital in Pietermaritzburg, a large town about 45 kilometres from the farm. That night I spoke to the family.

"Dad doesn't have long," I said. "Can we all fast and pray for him this evening, that he will open his heart to the Lord?"

The next day I drove in to see Dad at the hospital. I had made up my mind to have one more try to talk to

Angus with some of his miraculous potato crop, which he planted in faith against the advice of all his farming friends.

Angus and a few farm workers built this house in the traditional Zulu way, with wooden posts, mud bricks and a cement coating. Almost 30 years later – with some improvements – it is still the Buchans' home.

The farm entrance. When Angus and Jill named their farm Shalom, meaning "peace", they had no idea that God was leading them towards the extensive work of preaching, teaching, healing, fellowship and care that is now Shalom Ministries.

Angus and his father worked together to build the thatched chapel on the farm. It has become the focus of prayer and worship for the whole community at Shalom.

The twelve-metre cross beside the chapel was given in memory of a young man who died in a road accident. It is illuminated at night, and used as a beacon by light aircraft. The Shalom cross is visible for miles, bearing testimony to the Lord Jesus Christ.

Angus is proud to wear a kilt in the Buchan tartan, a gift from Robert Buchan in Scotland. For him it is proof that God is interested in the most trivial details of our lives, and delights to satisfy the desires of our hearts if we serve him (Psalm 37:4)

Little Alistair Buchan, who died in an accident on the farm. His short life has touched the hearts of thousands of people, as Angus has told the story of how the Lord upheld him through the darkest time of his life.

Simeon Bengu, the farm foreman, helped Angus carve out the farmland from overgrown scrub. He is a treasured brother in Christ, and supports Angus in prayer whenever he leaves the farm on a preaching campaign.

Once again Angus and his farm workers defy farming advice by planting in the dust and trusting God for the rain.

Their faith is rewarded and sufficient rain falls to enable the seed to germinate and begin to grow.

Another bumper crop on Shalom farm

Angus and his wife Jill with one of the orphans at the dedication of the children's home at Shalom. The children are cared for in body, mind and spirit, with good food and a safe, loving home; a small school on the farm; and the Shalom fellowship which surrounds them with prayer and shares the gospel with them as they grow.

Playtime at the children's home: some of the children showing their energy and exuberance as they play with Mandy Porée.

Thousands of people come to hear Angus preach his simple, powerful and uncompromising gospel message: that Jesus is Lord, and he has the power to forgive sins, heal the sick and offer new life to everyone.

Big evangelistic campaigns need equipment: power, lighting and amplification systems. Angus has solved the problems of reaching out to rural areas with the Seed Sower, a 20-tonne truck. It can carry the team into the heart of Africa, bringing the seed of God's word into places where the gospel has never been preached.

The auditorium at Shalom farm, built by faith and providing a venue for large meetings and conferences

Angus travels the world and preaches and teaches extensively, but his heart is with his family and fellowship on Shalom farm in Greytown. He loves to saddle his horse, Blaze, and ride around the farm he calls his "green cathedral", thanking God for the beauty of his creation.

him about Jesus, but the devil was telling me to give it up.

"Don't be a fool!" he said in my thoughts. "He's not interested. He never has been. Your dad will never change."

The Lord Jesus had made a promise to me. "I will give you your heart's desire." That was good enough for me. I decided to trust in the promise of God, not the lies of the devil. As I parked in the hospital car park I bowed my head. "Master, I only ask one favour," I said. "When I get to the ward, don't let anyone else be there. Only Dad and me." I thought that might make it easier for Dad to respond to what I had to say.

However, the Lord has a sense of humour! When I got to the ward, it was full of people: every other patient had a crowd of visitors.

Dad was propped up in bed, watching for me. My heart was filled with compassion for him as I saw my big strong father lying there. His curly hair was silver now, but his blue eyes were the same as ever. He'd brought me up to be a real South African man – reserved, strong, unemotional – but the words came to my lips: "Dad, I really love you." I'd never been able to say that before. I put my arms round him and gave him a hug.

"Dad, do you know you're dying?"

"I know that, Angus," he said.

"You need to make your peace with God."

There was a pause, then he said the words I'd been hoping for.

"Not before time, son."

I led him in the sinner's prayer. In front of all the

people in the ward, in his strong Scottish accent, he prayed after me: "Lord Jesus, I repent of all my sin. I ask you to be the Lord of my life from this day forward. Amen."

It was only then I became conscious of the silence that had fallen on the ward. People were wiping their eyes; one visitor came over and welcomed Dad into the family of the Lord; the nurses congratulated him. Suddenly there was a buzz of conversation, and a spirit of celebration filled the room as another soul came home.

I couldn't wait to get home to Jill and the children with the news. That afternoon we all gave thanks to Jesus for saving Dad.

Three weeks later, one sunny afternoon, George Buchan died peacefully. He went to be with his newly found Lord, and now he is home with his lovely wife and his grandson Alistair. My whole family have found the Lord and we know we will meet again in his presence. Alleluia.

6

A Greater Harvest

*I*t was a great joy to me that Dad had found Jesus; it was also another confirmation of the work God wanted me to do. A couple of years before Dad died I had been asked to speak to the young people in the church on the subject of divine healing, so I did some research. As I read about the mighty men and women whom God had blessed with this gift, I grew more and more excited. God showed me that those great Christians were just ordinary people who had dared to believe in his promises. They were Christians who had a hunger to see people come to salvation, the sick healed, the captives set free, the broken-hearted mended and families restored.

I had to share this revelation, so I called the pastor.

"That's right, Angus," he said. "God gives every one of us the power to do his will."

Suddenly I found myself telling him what was in my heart.

"I want to be used by God," I said. "I want to trust him at all costs and see his power manifested."

There was a pause on the other end of the line, and then the minister spoke thoughtfully.

"Angus," he said, "I believe that today is a very significant day in your life. I'm writing it up on the wall of my office as we speak – 17 November 1989. Be obedient to whatever the Lord puts into your heart."

That Friday night I spoke at the youth meeting and the Spirit of God seemed to be there with us in a special way. There were 50 or 60 young people there, and I talked about faith and shared my story with them. Like most youngsters they were hungry for a vision, and they could see what God could do through an ordinary farmer who was prepared to put his trust in Jesus. Many of them came to repentance and restoration that night, and we were awed as we witnessed God touching those young lives, healing them in body, mind and spirit.

I went home and told Jill what had happened. I knew it was the beginning of something that the Lord had in mind for my life.

Throughout November and December I continued to pray that God would use me. "What do you want me to do, Lord?" I felt ever more strongly that he was calling me to evangelise, but I found it hard to believe. I was only a farmer, not a trained preacher. "What do you want me to do, Lord?" I asked again.

That Christmas I bought Jill a beautiful Bible, with the words of the Lord printed in red. On Christmas Eve I was admiring it when one verse seemed to leap out at me. "Do not be afraid; keep on speaking, do not be silent" (Acts 18:9). It was the only verse in red on that entire page. I was sure that the Lord Jesus was calling me to preach.

Where should I start? We already prayed together

on the farm before work every morning, and I shared the word of God with my labourers, but now I sensed that God was calling me to a wider ministry.

"What do you want me to do, Lord?"

"I want you to preach the gospel. Trust me and you will see signs and wonders following the preaching of my word."

That sounded good to me. I would approach the pastor and ask him to let me preach in the church. I couldn't believe what the Lord said next.

"No, Angus, I don't want you to preach to church-goers. Hire a hall in Ladysmith. I want you to go to people who don't know me and share my word with them."

Hire a hall? I had never done that before. Preach at a gospel campaign? That would be a complete change for this farmer. But there was only one possible answer.

"Right, Lord. I'll do it if you say so."

Early one morning in January 1990, I set off for Ladysmith. I went in the farm pickup truck, wearing my usual khaki working clothes. I wasn't pretending to be anything other than I was – an ordinary farmer. It was a wonderful morning, and I sang as I drove down the long, straight road to Ladysmith. It was a two-hour drive, and as I went I began to hear a familiar voice.

"Who do you think you are, planning an evangelistic campaign? You're not even a preacher, just an illiterate farmer. Who do you think will want to come and listen to you?"

The old feelings of self-doubt, unworthiness and

plain fear began to fill my heart. Should I turn back? Was I deceiving myself?

"Drive on," said the Lord. His peace came into my heart.

I parked in the centre of Ladysmith, wondering how I would set about hiring a hall.

"Wait a minute," said the Lord. "I have three questions for you, Angus, before you carry on."

He had my full attention.

"Are you prepared to be a fool for me?"

That was easy to answer. It wouldn't be a new experience for me – I'm used to putting my foot in it. "Yes, Lord."

"Are you prepared for people to say all manner of evil about you for my sake?"

"Yes, I'm prepared for that."

"Are you prepared to see less of your family?"

I was silent. As a farmer I was used to coming home at night to be with the family. I've always taken it for granted – spending time at home with Jill and the children was my way of life. This was a decision I couldn't take lightly: God knew it would be a real sacrifice for me, but he would only send me if I was willing to go all the way with him.

"Yes, Lord. I'll drink this cup of sacrifice, but I can only do it by your grace."

I looked around me. I was standing right outside the town hall, so I went inside and asked the lady at the counter if she could help me. I was afraid she might laugh when I told her I wanted to book a hall for an evangelistic campaign, but she opened up the big desk diary.

"We have only one week available during April,"
she said, "except for the Saturday night – that's
already been booked."

"I'll take it."

I felt on top of the world. I'd done it! Angus
Buchan, a farmer called by God, would be running a
week's evangelistic campaign in Ladysmith. I set off
for home, filled with the excitement of doing something for God.

"What about the Saturday, Lord?" I asked as I
drove. Just then the large army barracks came into
view: "5th South African Infantry" said the sign outside. The Holy Spirit prompted me to turn into the
entrance. I was stopped by the guards on the gate.

"I want to see the general," I said boldly.

"The *kommandant*," corrected one of them.

"Fine. I'll see him."

I filled in some papers and they let me in. Within a
few minutes, with no appointment or recommenda-
tion, I found myself facing the *kommandant*.

"How can I help you?" he asked.

In those days South Africa had a policy of conscrip-
tion: every white South African male over the age of
18 had to serve for two years in the army. My own eldest son, Andy, had recently been called up and was
away from home for the first time. We missed him
badly.

"Sir, I have a son of my own in the army, and I know
what these boys are going through. I want to come
and encourage them about Jesus."

"Fine," said the *kommandant*. "We'll have 500 troops
at the Elands Hall on the Saturday night."

My heart seemed to skip a beat. I had never preached to more than about 80 people in church. Now I had let myself in for preaching to 500! I thanked him profusely and went home in a daze.

With only three months to prepare for the campaign, Jill and I talked about what we needed to do.

"We must share the vision with the local churches and submit to their leadership," I said. However, my visits to the church leaders in Ladysmith were a disappointment. The first minister I met was unenthusiastic.

"The people of Ladysmith are just like the rocks and thorn trees of the area – hard and dry," he said. "You'll get nowhere with them." At least he promised to tell his people about the campaign.

At the next church the young pastor listened to what I said. "Well, you can come if you want to, but in my opinion this town has been over-evangelised." I could hardly believe my ears. Surely if there was one soul left unsaved, there was room for the gospel?

My next call was to a church with a reputation for liveliness. Surely here I would find support.

"Three months ago," said the pastor, "two of South Africa's top evangelists held a campaign here. The first night only 39 people came to the meeting, and 18 of those were from my own church. Tell me, who are your main speakers?"

I hesitated. "Well, I am. In fact, I'm the only speaker!"

His face was a picture. "Well, brother, maybe the Lord has sent you here ... to bend you a little."

I felt totally humiliated and disillusioned. When I

called on the last minister it was quite a relief to find that he wasn't at home. I drove out of town with a heavy heart. I had planned to book accommodation for the team in a local motel, but I could hardly bear to carry on. I parked the pickup truck under a tree outside the motel and cried out to God.

"Lord, why do you want me to do this?" It seemed to me that there was a church on every corner in Ladysmith, and not one of their ministers wanted me to come. Still, I had promised the Lord, so I would go through with it. I went in and booked the rooms in blind faith.

That evening, just as we were about to sit down to dinner, the phone rang. It was Brian Jubber, the minister who had been out. His voice was full of excitement.

"I have to come and see you urgently. We've been praying for six months for revival and asking the Lord to send us an evangelist! We'll be with you first thing in the morning!"

Jill and I were overwhelmed at the goodness of God: at last we had some support, and it was such a joy and encouragement. Brian and his church worked hard; they organised a Men's Breakfast, they put up banners and posters around the town, and they upheld us in prayer.

Gradually the team began to come together. We were a small, inexperienced group of ordinary people, nervous about what we had taken on, but determined to do God's will. We loved the Lord Jesus and were prepared to fulfil his Great Commission, to go into the world and preach the gospel to everyone.

The first precious brother God gave me was Steyn

du Preez, a young man from Zimbabwe who was managing a farm in the Greytown area. He is a great prayer warrior, and every week he and I would meet to pray for the campaign. Those times of prayer became very important to me, strengthening us all for the tests that lay ahead – prayer is a very powerful weapon against the evil one. Steyn went on to become one of my greatest friends, and I thank God for bringing him into my life.

We knew that we needed to advertise our campaign, with handbills, posters and newspaper adverts, and the Lord sent us some assistance in the form of my brother-in-law, John Collier, an advertising man. My sister Morag had given her life to the Lord, but John was still a man of the world. All the same, he was willing to help us and offered to come and video the whole campaign. Morag was delighted.

Ian Corbridge, Jill's brother, flew up from Port Elizabeth to lead our music. A talented guitarist, Ian writes challenging Christian songs. He has been a committed Christian since the age of fifteen, and I had always admired him for his uncompromising stand for the Lord. Back in the days when I was a wild young rugby player the team would always go into the bar after a game and have a few beers, but Ian was happy to sit on the veranda and drink Coca-Cola. His consistent testimony made a great impression on me. Now he was married and qualified as a maths and physical education teacher, but he made time to come and help us at Ladysmith; in the years that followed, his music was to have a profound effect on our work at Shalom.

Our pastor Gavin was to play the piano, and his wife Jean would sing and help another young woman, Karen, with the ministry. Buddy was our drummer and sound man.

None of us had ever done anything like this before; all we knew was that Jesus Christ is faithful, and that was enough for us. We set off for Ladysmith.

The first meeting was scheduled to begin at 7 p.m., and at 6.50 the hall was empty except for the music team on the platform, singing for all they were worth. I went down to the basement to pray.

"Lord, we have a covenant," I said. "We've done all we can. The rest is up to you."

I went upstairs again and peeped into the hall – it was half full.

That night set the pattern for the whole campaign. We opened with the music team, who led us in praise and worship. Then I got up and preached. My message was short, punchy, fiery and challenging, about our need to get back to God and a life of holiness. There's only one way to live our lives for Jesus, and there can be no half-measures: we can't serve two masters. I'm an evangelist, not a teacher, so although I preach from the Bible I use lots of everyday illustrations, too. I also stride around the stage a lot – I'm a man of the wide open spaces, and I feel too boxed-in in a pulpit!

Then we sang a meditative hymn, "Just as I am", and I called forward all the people who wanted to serve Jesus Christ with all their hearts. I don't go in for closed eyes or bowed heads: if anyone wants to serve the Lord, they have to come right out and do it in front of their neighbours and their friends. It takes courage to stand up in front of the whole town and come forward, and I came down from the stage to meet them, and led them in the sinner's prayer.

"Dear Lord Jesus, I acknowledge that I'm a sinner. I repent of my sin, and ask you to come into my life and make a fresh start. I thank you that Jesus died for me on Calvary and rose again for my salvation. Thank you for saving me from depression, fear and sin; thank you for living in me and giving me a brand-new opportunity to live for you. Amen."

That first night six people came forward, and I met them with joy at the front of the hall, new brothers and sisters in Christ. I hadn't actually been expecting anyone to respond, but after all, it wasn't my message but God's, and he knew the hearts he wanted to reach. By the end of the week, 50 or 60 people were coming forward each night.

Then we invited people to come forward for prayer. On the Wednesday evening Jill was praying with a lady who wanted Jesus to help her stop smoking. Somehow my wife sensed that this woman had deeper needs, and called me over to join them. The woman looked up at me anxiously. "I have a tumour on the brain," she told me. "Tomorrow I go for a scan."

"Can I tell these people?" I asked her.

"What have I got to lose?" she replied.

I could feel that the hearts of all those in the hall were drawn to this woman as we prayed the prayer of faith together, asking God to heal her. "Come back and tell us the results of the scan," I called after her as she walked away.

On Thursday I didn't see her anywhere, and my

heart sank. Maybe God hadn't healed her; maybe I had given her a false hope. Then I noticed a woman walking towards me, followed by her husband and children. She was smiling radiantly, and looked so different that I hadn't recognised her.

"The scan was clear!" she said. "I am completely healed!" All around the hall people began to thank God and to shout his praises. It was a wonderful moment.

At the end of the week the team gathered in the motel for the last time. We were sorry that the campaign was over and our last meeting was finished – we were so filled with excitement at what the Lord had done, after such an unpromising start. He had one more surprise for us.

"What about you, John?" I asked my brother-in-law, who had been filming every meeting.

To my amazement I saw that he had tears in his eyes.

"I couldn't come forward, because I was filming," he said. "But every night I've prayed the sinner's prayer with you."

"Why not do it now?" I suggested, and right there and then he knelt down in that motel room and asked the Lord Jesus Christ to come into his heart and be Lord of his life.

There was only one final event to organise: Saturday night at the army camp. The *kommandant* had promised us 500 young men, and as we turned in at the gate I wondered if they would all be there.

The meeting was due to begin at 7 p.m., and at 6.30 I looked into the hall. The 500 soldiers were already seated, and as we watched, company after company was being marched across the parade ground and in at the doors. There wasn't going to be room for them all: an officer told them to take out the chairs and sit on the floor. In the end about 1,300 young soldiers were squashed in the hall. It was the biggest crowd I had ever spoken to.

The plan was that the format should follow the Ladysmith meetings, but it didn't work out like that. It was Saturday night – their night off – and instead of being out on the town and getting stuck into the beer, these young lads had been commanded by their officers to go and listen to a preacher! They were hunched or sprawled on the floor, some glaring at me with daggers in their eyes. Conscripted into the army against their will, now they'd been conscripted into my meeting!

My son Andy was stationed at Tempe, a huge military base near Blomfontein, about a day and a half's drive away; he had managed to get a weekend pass and had hitch-hiked down to hear me speak. I could see him sitting at the back of the hall. The music team tried to sing one or two songs but they were making no headway; no one was joining in. These lads weren't interested.

I looked out at those young men and my heart was filled with compassion for them. Like Andy, they were homesick, a long way from home, and trying to make the best of the new life they'd been thrust into. Like a word from the Holy Spirit the thoughts came into my head. These youngsters had all been uprooted from everything that was familiar to them, and they came from every kind of background – town and country, rich and poor, Christians and unbelievers. Peer pressure at this age is tremendous. What challenges were they facing in their young lives?

I stepped forward and started to speak to them on a personal level, like a father to a son. "Without Jesus you will never make it on your own. There are so many dangers out there. Without him you will end up on the side of the road, all washed up." As I spoke I could see a change in their body language. They unfolded their arms, they stopped looking angry and defensive, and they began to listen. The Holy Spirit had already started to work in their hearts.

I had seen the Spirit working in Ladysmith, night after night, and I knew he could do the same here.

"We're going to give you the opportunity to stand up and make a public confession of your faith before everyone here," I told them. "If you mean business with God, with everyone watching, get to your feet."

I'll never forget what happened next. A big strong soldier right at the back got up. He stood at ease, shoulders back and head held high, as if defying the world. There was silence. Then another soldier stood, and another and another. It reminded me of a field of ripe wheat being blown by a gentle breeze as the Holy Spirit blew through the Elands Hall. I was stunned. A thousand young men were standing before me.

"Wait a minute. This is no time to play games. You have to count the cost of following Jesus. If you don't mean it, please sit down." No one moved.

"Listen," I scolded them. "It's a terrible thing to fall into the hands of the living God. You are giving him control of your life. Only stand if you really want to give your life to Jesus Christ."

Still no one sat down. The Holy Spirit spoke in my heart. "I am doing this work, not you. Just be the obedient vessel I called you to be."

"Men," I said softly, "let's pray."

The memory of those 1,000 young soldiers saying the sinner's prayer together will live in my heart for ever. Together we sang, "He is Lord", and they lifted their heads and their strong young voices filled the hall. It's a picture I will take to heaven with me. It was proof, yet again, that God honours his children. When you step out in faith, God opens the door of blessing.

We handed out all the follow-up material and decision cards we had, and when we got home that night, every last piece of literature we had prepared for the campaign had gone. God had taken our efforts for him and turned them into something wonderful. I don't think any of us slept much that night, tired as we were. We were all rejoicing in God's faithfulness and the great harvest of souls he had gathered in.

I knew then that the Lord of the harvest had called me to a new field. From now on, running the farm would only be a means to an end. I promised I would do as the Lord had asked: preach the gospel at every opportunity, pray for the sick, heal the brokenhearted and set the captives free in the name of Jesus.

Life would never be the same again.

7
Planting in the Dust

*T*he Lord was true to his promise: other campaigns followed after Ladysmith, and however nervous and inadequate I felt before them, always the Holy Spirit would show me what to say. "At that time you will be given what to say, for it will not be you speaking, but the Spirit of your Father speaking through you" (Matthew 10:19 - 20).

In October 1992 we hired the New Farmers' Hall in Newcastle, northern KwaZulu-Natal, about three hours' drive north-east of Greytown. The hall could seat around 3,000 people, and it was filled to capacity every night.

We had been to farmers' meetings in the area, and they had agreed to arrange transport for us. They hired buses and used their own vehicles to bring people in from their farms and from the townships. There was a festive feeling as the convoys of trucks and buses rolled into town, with the dust rising from the wheels and the people sitting in the back singing. It's a wonderful thing to hear the Zulu people singing – they would give the Welsh some competition!

There was a spirit of great expectation in the air. The people were hungry for God.

Inside the hall we had a big band, with piano, guitars, trumpets and drums, so we made a joyful noise to the Lord. Then I told them about the death of my nephew Alistair and the incredible grace of God that had upheld me in the darkest time of my life. There was utter silence. The death of a child is a universal thing – everyone can feel your pain. It touched people's hearts that God could get me through that experience, and it made them realise what he could do for them.

One night I talked about Jesus being on trial before Pontius Pilate.

"You are the crowd watching him," I told them. "What are you going to do with Jesus? Mary Magdalene is screaming, 'Let him go!' Pilate, a heathen man, is saying, 'Give him a chance!' Everywhere people are shouting, 'Crucify him!' What about you? Are you agreeing to his death by the hypocrisy of your lifestyle and the sin in your life? Or will you stand up for Jesus tonight?"

As I made the altar call over a thousand people stood up. Many were weeping as they repented and made a decision to receive Jesus Christ as their Lord and Saviour. I knew that the Lord was doing great things in the hearts and lives of these people. We had counsellors waiting to receive them, and after that we went on for another two hours, praying for the sick, the demon-possessed, the lost, the lonely and the unemployed. We prayed the prayer of faith for everyone who asked, because Jesus meets people at their point of need, whether it's healing for physical illness or the touch of love and hope for a life that's in despair.

On the way home from Newcastle I was rejoicing at the work the Lord had done. I was in a hurry to get back to the farm, because it was the planting season, and the campaign had held me up. We were almost a week behind schedule, and I knew all the other farmers would already be busy in their fields.

However, as we approached Greytown I looked around in astonishment. There was no sign of farming activity, and the fields were empty. Even an inexperienced eye could have seen the reason: they were also dry. The rains hadn't come, and no one had been able to plough, let alone start planting.

The next morning I went to my office as usual to spend time with the Lord.

"I'm not complaining, Lord, but you know what we've been doing these last few days. We've been bringing in the harvest of souls as you told us to. I thought that when I got back it would at least be raining."

I looked out of the window. There wasn't a cloud in the sky. It wasn't even hot enough to set off a thunderstorm.

A farmer has to be a businessman. In a way, so does an evangelist: a major evangelistic campaign needs finance. In this matter as in all others, I believe in the faithfulness of God to enable us to do his will. "And my God will meet all your needs according to his glorious riches in Christ Jesus" (Philippians 4:19). I was determined never to ask for money, never to send out begging "newsletters", and never to appeal for offerings.

The apostle Paul was a tent-maker, and he earned his living in that way. I am a farmer, and my occupation supports me, so that I don't have to ask God's faithful people to give me money.

When we ran our campaign in the Transvaal one of our helpers invited an old farmer, but he wasn't interested.

"All evangelists are money-makers," he said.

"This one isn't," came the reply. "He doesn't even take up a collection." The farmer came along to see this phenomenon and found Jesus.

In those early days of the gospel campaigns I was paying for everything from my own pocket, and I had to dig deep for advertising, posters, accommodation for the team and hiring the hall. The farm was my only source of income, and over the years, Shalom has poured a small fortune into the ministry. Nowadays we are helped by some voluntary giving, but the farm still subsidises 90 per cent of the ministry.

God has always supplied all our needs through the farm, and as our ministry has developed, through books, television and radio programmes, campaigns and the growing community at Shalom, his generosity has never let us down. All the same, that year, like any farmer, I was concerned about the prospects for the crops in such a dry spring.

As I pondered all this, I heard footsteps outside the door. It was Simeon, coming as usual for our time of prayer before starting work.

"*Sawubona, mfewethu* (Greetings, brother)," I said.

"How was Newcastle?" asked Simeon.

"Jesus was faithful as always," I replied. "There

were miracles of healing, and many people found the Lord."

Simeon beamed from ear to ear – he has the warmest smile I have ever seen.

"That is good news," he said. "*Nkosi* (the King) is great."

"But Simeon, what's been happening here?" I asked. "Everything is so dry. The other farmers aren't doing any planting. There's no sign of movement on any of the other farms. What are we going to do? We're losing time."

"*Aka lutu, mfewethu*," he replied. "It doesn't matter."

"It doesn't matter? Simeon, this is serious!"

"Look," he said, "let's go and plant the crop. We're late already."

"Simeon, you don't have to be an agricultural graduate to know you don't plant seed into dry ground! You wait for the rain to fall first."

The big Zulu looked me straight in the eye. His voice was filled with authority and complete conviction.

"Brother, you have just come back from a mighty revival, and you have seen God move with signs and miracles each day. Can you not trust him to bring rain on our maize crops? Why are you not prepared to plant in the dust and believe Jesus to bring the rain?"

I was rebuked. I asked the Lord – and Simeon – to forgive me for my lack of faith.

"You're right. Let's go and get the tractors and the maize planter out. Load up the big trailer with fertiliser, hitch up the discs and ploughs, and we'll get rolling."

It was quite a sight to see the big convoy of tractors

and equipment going down to the maize fields. The earth was so dry you could see the dust rising for miles around. I'm sure the other farmers were thinking we had really gone over the top this time. We worked hard all day, and when we had finished, I looked around the fields.

"Here it is, Lord. Your crop of maize. This may be the worst season we've ever experienced. If you give us the best crop we've ever had, then I'll know for definite that you have called me to preach the gospel full time. I will release the entire farming operation into your hands." It was a solemn vow, a covenant with the Lord.

We have never prayed a crop through as we did that one. We would get a few drops of rain, just enough to germinate the seed, then the sky would clear again. I watched the shoots struggling to push up through the baked ground, slowly twisting and turning white.

"Lord!" I would call. "Your crop is dying!"

Just in time a little more rain would fall.

Some of the other farmers in the district had decided to wait for the rains before planting, and as a result they planted late and ended up with a very poor crop. I think we had more calluses on our knees than on our hands as our miracle crop continued growing, slowly but surely.

Andrew had finished his time in the army and was now at university studying agriculture. He came home that summer to find us both exhausted, and he persuaded us to go away for a few days. The crop was standing knee high, at a crucial stage in its growth, but there was nothing we could do. It was up to the Lord. We left Andy in charge of the farm.

Andy loves the Lord, and every morning he went to my office for his prayer time, asking for God's blessing on our work and rain for the maize. One day he was out in the fields, looking at the dusty earth, when he saw black rain clouds gathering. As the drops of rain began to fall he jumped out of the truck in excitement, praising God, but at once a strong east wind blew up and the storm moved away.

Andy was devastated. He could see the rain falling in the distance, but our farm was as dry as ever. Back indoors he opened his Bible and prayed.

"Lord, what's happening? Dad and Mum are serving you with all their hearts. All the profits from this crop are going into the preaching of the gospel. Why are we suffering this drought?"

Then he looked down at the Bible on his lap. It was open at Ecclesiastes 11:4. He could hardly believe what he was reading. "Whoever watches the wind will not plant; whoever looks at the clouds will not reap."

"Sorry, Lord," he said. "Forgive me for not trusting you."

The next morning when he woke up a cold front had moved in, and a gentle, persistent rain was falling.

We all learned valuable lessons from that crop. The Lord showed us the importance of walking by faith, and not by sight, of trusting him unconditionally and never giving up. At the end of the season we reaped five tonnes of seed per hectare. Most of the maize stalks had two cobs on them, and sometimes even three. It was the best crop I had ever harvested, and truly miraculous for a drought year. Farmers and friends came to look at the fields and gazed in amazement. All the praise and glory went to the supreme farmer, King Jesus. Everyone knew this could only have been a miracle.

We serve a covenant-keeping God. He always keeps his side of the agreement and expects us to keep ours. I bowed my head with thanksgiving and determined to keep my part of the vow. The farm would serve the Lord, and so would I.

This experience taught me to trust the Lord with my livelihood as well as my life. Peter was a fisherman, and when he needed money to pay the temple tax, Jesus told him to go to the lake and throw out his line. "Take the first fish you catch; open its mouth and you will find a four-drachma coin" (Matthew 17:27). The same has held true for me: the coin is in the fish's mouth. God has made me a fisher of men. As long as I am preaching the gospel, the money comes in. When I stop preaching, the money drops. God knows exactly how much I need to pay for his work.

God has called me to the office of evangelist, and the tools of the trade are signs and wonders. We shouldn't be surprised when miracles happen. Time and again, the Lord has put faith in my heart to trust him for a miracle, and the result has always been a harvest of souls for the kingdom of God. Too many evangelists preach about theories and ideas: we preach a down-to-earth gospel of faith in action.

This is especially true when it comes to healing the sick. We always make time for prayer for healing at the end of our gospel meetings, and it is a major part of our ministry. We do it because Jesus healed the sick, and because it is part of his Great Commission: "Go into all the world and preach the good news to all creation. Whoever believes and is baptised will be saved, but whoever does not believe will be condemned. And these signs will accompany those who believe ... they will place their hands on sick people, and they will get well" (Mark 16:15–18).

This is the basis of my understanding of the prayer for healing. I believe in the inspiration of scripture, and like the evangelist Smith Wigglesworth, I claim, "God said it – I believe it – and that settles it!" We anoint people with oil as a symbol of the Holy Spirit, and ask for the power of God's healing in the name of the Trinity, Father, Son and Holy Spirit. Testimonies continually pour into the office as the Lord saves and heals people from all over the country. Every testimony encourages me more to work for Jesus and do the will of the Father.

Friends brought Heinz Baum to Shalom when he developed ME (myalgic encephalomyelitis) after a bout of glandular fever. He was too weak to work, and the doctor had prescribed medication and bed rest. His company director had recommended that he take early retirement because of ill health. I anointed him with oil and we prayed together. A few days later, Heinz telephoned me.

"As we drove home I felt a sensation in the centre of my forehead," he said. "It was as if there was a source of heat which was penetrating my head. I didn't tell anyone and just went to bed as usual. In the morning the sensation was gone, and so was the dark tunnel I had been experiencing, and the awful tiredness. When Dr Shearer examined me again, he said he couldn't understand it but all the symptoms of ME had gone."

Alta Kilian wrote from Durnacol. "Just a short note to let you know that I am fine after hands were laid on me during a service at the Iscor Club at Durnacol during August last year. I had Parkinson's disease as well as cancer. I give thanks to God that I am still alive and living a normal life."

Alan Draper, captain of a 2,000-tonne cargo ship, shared his dramatic story with us. His ship went aground on a reef during a gale, and during the subsequent salvage operation he suffered a horrific accident. His right arm was caught in a winch line and crushed against a steel bulkhead. His wrist and hand were crushed and his elbow and shoulder shattered. He was taken to a nearby hospital for emergency surgery and warned that he should not expect to regain the use of his right hand. But Alan was a believer.

"Even though I had been given pain-killing drugs, I was alert enough to reject the words the doctor spoke over me. I remembered the promise in Jeremiah 30:17: 'I will restore you to health and heal your wounds, declares the Lord.'"

Alan's healing was limited. His wrist had set at an angle of 45 degrees and would not move; he had only partial movement in his elbow and shoulder, and because the nerve was severed his right arm began to wither. It was in this condition that he attended one of our meetings.

"My hope in the word was still alive," he said, "and I responded when you urged me to come to the altar for prayer. As you laid your hands on my bent, misshapen arm, I felt the anointing of God flow through it. That solid mass of fused bones became soft; my wrist and fingers straightened out before my eyes, and as you held my arm above my head, my elbow became straight. I couldn't stop praising God."

The neurosurgeon has subsequently confirmed that the nerves in his arm have been restored; he has been declared fit to resume his normal duties.

Many people come to us for healing because they simply can't afford to go to a doctor, even if one is available. We are constantly awed by the work that the Lord does among them. We have seen people throw away their crutches and walk; others take out their hearing aids and respond to the sound of their name being called; I have seen two men get out of their wheelchairs and stand tall.

One of these men had been shot in the spine by a policeman several years earlier. Before I prayed with him I asked, "Do you forgive the man who did this to you?" He looked at me with big eyes and said, "Yes." I had no doubt he was telling the truth. We prayed together and he got up and walked out of the hall, praising the God who honours the prayer of faith.

There is an obvious question: what of the people who are not healed? Why do some people receive healing and see God perform miracles in their lives, and others have to battle on with illness or disability? My answer is the same as the one Katherine Kuhlman gave to the journalist who asked her a similar question. "I don't know. When I get to heaven one day I'll ask Jesus, and he'll tell me. But until then, I'll continue laying on hands and praying in faith, and expecting the Lord to heal the sick and set the afflicted free."

We are told that healing is a natural part of the life of the church of Jesus: "Is any one of you sick? He should call the elders of the church to pray over him and anoint him with oil in the name of the Lord. And the prayer offered in faith will make the sick person well; the Lord will raise him up. If he has sinned, he will be forgiven. Therefore confess your sins to each other and pray for each other so that you may be healed. The prayer of a righteous man is powerful and effective" (James 5:14–16).

Back home on the farm, every Thursday we have a service in the chapel especially for people coming for physical healing or inner healing and deliverance. They come from far and wide – people have flown for two hours from Cape Town, or driven for three or four hours in a pickup truck, just to attend. It's part of the life of Shalom. The farm not only supports our mission financially; it also plays a fundamental role in our mission to preach the gospel, becoming a centre for the healing and wholeness of body, mind and spirit.

The little services of praise and worship which I started out holding under a tree with a few Zulu workers are now held in our beautiful chapel, Bethel, built on the highest part of the farm. We have a regular congregation of around 200 people. Each year we run a Mighty Men conference, for around 600 men. They love to come to the farm and spend time there in the beauty and peace of the countryside and the warm fellowship of our community.

The farm is also a good teacher: there are lessons to be learned from farming which have parallels in our spiritual lives for those who have eyes to see them. I call the Bible "the farmer's handbook" because it uses so many farming analogies. Jesus lived in a rural community, and many of the descriptions he uses relate closely to our life here. When he wants to teach us the lesson of perseverance, he says, "No one who puts his hand to the plough and looks back is fit for service in the kingdom of God" (Luke 9:62). Farmers understand that kind of language.

If you spend any time working on the land you can see the sense of it immediately. When you are ploughing you fix your eye on a point on the horizon, set the plough into the ground behind you, put the tractor in gear and set off. A man looking backwards cannot plough in a straight line. If you begin to doubt yourself and wonder if the plough has gone in deep enough, or if it lifted out halfway down the field, you will be tempted to turn your head to check. The moment you do that, you put a kink in the first line you plough, and once that kink is there, it grows. When you turn at the end of the field and come back, the wheel goes into the furrow you made, and at every turn the kink gets bigger. By the time you have finished, you have a big lazy curve in the middle of your field. If you allow one little sin to creep into your life, and think it doesn't matter, it will grow and grow until it affects your whole spiritual life, deflecting you from your primary aim of serving God.

Jesus knew that, long before tractors were invented. That's why he said when we put our hand to the plough – when we make our decision to follow him all the way – we must not look behind us. This has happened to so many people who started out with God in faith. They took their eyes off the Lord and the vision he gave them, and the work failed.

It's true that we are all weak and sometimes we don't feel that we are achieving as much as we would like for the Lord, but he is the one who is the judge of our work. One year I planted a crop of maize but it didn't germinate properly. The gaps between the plants were so big that I could walk through the field in the early morning without getting any dew on my clothes. If you have a proper crop density, that should be impossible. I had to tend that field, weed it and fertilise it, but I used to get so discouraged. Every time I looked at it, my heart sank.

Then one day the Holy Spirit spoke to my heart. "Stop looking at the gaps in the field," he said. "Start looking at the maize." When I did, my whole outlook changed. I realised that the cobs were gigantic because they had no competition and they could make the most of the fertiliser and water they were getting. That year we had a severe drought, but because of my low plant population I was able to reap a respectable yield, and make a good profit. Once again, I had to persevere in the work the Lord had given me to do, ignoring all distractions and discouragements, and fix my eyes on God and his promises.

For the Christian, faith should not be a "one-off" event. We must walk by faith every day in every area of our lives. When someone asks us what God has done for us, we shouldn't be recounting something that happened 20 years ago. Faith is a day-to-day lifestyle and experience of Jesus Christ. That's what we are experiencing at Shalom, when we plant in faith – even in the dust – and trust in him for the miracles of his love.

8
God's Provision

*T*he Newcastle campaign of 1992 was pivotal for us in several ways. One evening in a meeting there I spoke about a deep desire of my heart: I longed to be able to visit Scotland and preach the gospel. It was my parents' homeland and the place where I had done my agricultural training, and I felt a burden for the Scottish people.

Although I didn't know it, a young Scottish missionary was in the audience. She wrote a letter to her family in the south-west of Scotland, telling them about our evangelistic work and the Farmers for Jesus campaign, and they were fired by the vision that I could speak to the farmers of Scotland. When I got home I found an air letter waiting for me. A young man called Sandy Jamieson would arrange a preaching itinerary for me across Scotland, if I could make my way there.

It was an answer to prayer and an exciting prospect, but how could such a trip be financed? I was sure that God was in these plans, and I knew I could trust him to provide a way. The answer came swiftly and simply. A young Christian couple visited the farm, and as they were leaving they handed me an envelope.

"This is for your trip to Britain," they said. I thanked them, thinking it was a card wishing me a safe trip. When I opened it later on, my heart nearly stopped. Inside was a cheque for R10,000, more than enough for my air fare to Scotland.

However, there was still one other problem: the tour Sandy had organised for me would take nine weeks – too long for me to be away from the farm.

That year we had enjoyed two exceptional harvests: of souls won for Jesus in the Newcastle campaign, and of mealies on the farm. Now I knew beyond a shadow of doubt that the Lord had called me into full-time ministry, and that it would require my total commitment. Jill and I were facing one of the hardest tests we had known: we were placing on the altar everything we loved and had worked so hard for. We surrendered everything to God.

"Lord, we are in your hands. Shalom belongs to you." It was the base for our ministry and the source of our finance.

Invitations for evangelism were becoming more and more frequent, and they involved a lot more work than I had realised at first. We needed to visit the local churches, book venues, organise accommodation for team members, take care of advertising and prepare the talks and sermons for the meetings. We were finding it increasingly impossible to meet the demands of the farm at the same time. At home we were running a herd of beef cattle, growing our crops of seed maize and caring for the pine plantation. I was struggling to balance my two callings, and I couldn't be in two places at once.

"How can I leave the farm? Who will take care of it? Please send someone, Lord."

As I prayed, a young couple came into my mind. Steyn and Carol du Preez were good friends. I had become very close to Steyn when we prayed together for the Ladysmith campaign, and I knew he was a man of God. He was employed as a farm manager by the Pioneer Seed Company, and he had won the Champion Farmer title twice in the previous few years. He was ideally suited to manage Shalom and become a working partner. I asked him to pray about it.

A couple of days later he called to see me.

"I'm prepared to come and help you, Angus," he said. "I believe this is what the Lord is calling me to do." I marvelled at the grace of God and the willingness of this young man to put aside his farming career to release me for my work as an evangelist.

I was keen to make sure the farm was in good heart for Steyn to take over, but I was busy preparing for the trip to Scotland. We usually entered the local fat stock show, and we had won on a number of occasions, but this year I decided to give it a miss. However, we're part of a busy and friendly farming community. It's a good cattle area and the competition is keen, and the locals weren't going to let us get away with backing out.

"Come on, Angus, you have to enter," they said. "We won't take no for an answer!"

I agreed reluctantly. "I'll just enter three animals," I said. Normally I entered about fourteen.

I didn't have much time to prepare the three fat steers I selected for the show. I instructed the stockman to groom them regularly and make sure they ate and drank well, but that was the sum total of my preparation for the show. I was busy writing letters to Scotland and fixing dates and places for the preaching tour.

All the same, I took time out to attend the show, and as I settled back in my seat I looked around me with contentment. It seemed as if the whole of Greytown had turned out, and I smiled and nodded to friends around the ring. It didn't matter if we didn't win anything – at least I was here, taking part.

The stewards brought out the first batch of animals to be judged. I had one animal among about 30. The judges began to dismiss the inferior beasts one by one. Twenty were left – and mine was still there. Ten, six, four ... I began to get really excited. I was on the edge of my seat as the last few left the ring. One was left – our steer from Shalom! The crowd clapped as the winner was announced. We had qualified to compete in the Grand Champion section at the end of the show.

In round two the next batch of animals came in, and again we won. When it happened the third time I could hardly believe my eyes. Shalom had three animals in the final championship. I held my breath as the judges examined all the animals in the ring, but there was no hesitation: they unanimously voted one of ours the Grand Champion.

Not only did we take home awards for the best animals in their respective sections as well as the Grand Champion, but we were also awarded the trophy for the Stockman of the Show. God is so good. I knew that when Steyn took over, he would be managing a farm he could be proud of, and one of the best in the area.

We handed over the running of the farm at the end of autumn; the miracle crop we planted in the dust had been reaped and the fields were bare. Steyn and I made a covenant together in the sight of God and sealed it with the breaking of bread; he had complete authority to run the farm, and Jill and I trusted him completely. It was a fresh beginning for us all.

I said goodbye to our church in Greytown and promised to take their greetings to the church in Scotland. At the same time, I made them a promise that seemed symbolic of my attachment to my Scottish background.

"Psalm 37:4 says that the Lord will give us the desires of our heart if we serve him," I told them. "I know that our God is interested in the most trivial details of our lives. The one thing every true Scotsman wants to own is his own tartan, and I would love to have a kilt in the Buchan tartan. I can't afford to buy one – it would cost around £600! I am not even going to ask for one. But I believe that the Lord will give me one."

Perhaps it was a selfish request, but it was an honest one. The Lord knows what is in our hearts. He knew, too, how hard it was for me to leave the family. Our youngest daughter Jilly was only twelve, too young to be left without her parents for almost three months, so my wife had decided that she would stay at home with the children. However, our older daughter Lindi was 22, and we agreed that she would accompany me on the trip. It would be an opportunity for her to see the world, and also for us to spend time together.

As Lindi and I drove out of the farm gate that day, I was reminded of the Lord's challenge on the road to Ladysmith. "Are you prepared to see less of your family for the sake of the gospel?" Now I answered him again.

"Yes, Lord, but only by your grace."

We boarded the aircraft with great excitement and anticipation – we were really going to Scotland. It was a dream come true. At the same time I felt totally inadequate. Who was I, a simple farmer, to be going on a preaching tour of Scotland? I could only place my faith in Jesus, who never lets us down.

We landed at Heathrow and spent a couple of days with an old childhood friend of mine, who now lived in England. Then we caught a train to Dumfries where we were met by Sandy Jamieson and his wife Janice. They were wonderful people who had worked hard organising the tour. I thanked God for them.

We began to get a feeling for the land we were visiting. Scotland is a beautiful country, but it needs another John Knox. The people are warm and friendly, but they are self-sufficient: many of them don't feel that they need God. It was a shock to me. In the developing world the people are hungry for God. In central Africa, if you don't preach a two-hour sermon, they don't believe you're a preacher! I simply wasn't familiar with the kind of sermon where people start looking at their watches after fifteen minutes.

We had been invited to preach at all sorts of venues – churches, farmers' meetings, prisons and men's groups. In the mainstream churches they sang hymns;

in the charismatic churches they sang gospel songs; in the "Wee Free" churches they don't sing at all, but the Psalms are led by chanters. Often we would find the churches empty except for half a dozen white-haired old people in the front row. Nevertheless, we received a warm welcome everywhere.

The Lord blessed us in all sorts of ways. Malcolm MacPherson, an evangelist just back from Russia, came to see us, and parked his new four-litre Land Cruiser outside the house where we were staying.

"Use it as long as you need, Angus," he said as he gave me the keys. Lindi and I drove the length and breadth of Scotland in that vehicle. The Lord blessed our work: wherever we went, souls came to Christ; backsliders repented and came back to Jesus. What a faithful Lord we serve.

There was one problem: early in the trip I had hurt my back badly – ironically, swinging an axe to help chop logs for the fire, the sort of work I would think nothing of at home. I was in agony, and I seriously wondered whether I would have to call off the tour. The pain was so intense I could hardly walk, and lying on a soft bed was really uncomfortable. At night I would secretly take the blankets off the bed and sleep on the floor, then get up early and re-make the bed so as not to offend my hosts! I struggled on because I didn't want to let these good people down, and the amazing thing was that whenever I got up to preach, the pain would disappear.

I began to understand Paul's experience: he too had a thorn in his flesh, and when he cried out to God to remove it, the Lord's reply was always the same. His

grace was sufficient, and Paul's weakness demonstrated the Lord's strength. I could relate to that. In
spite of my difficulties, souls were being saved and the
sick were miraculously healed as God worked in their
lives. We learned many lessons in Scotland, and the
greatest was that we should not rely on our feelings;
we had to walk by faith and not by sight. So often,
when we are feeling discouraged and are about to give
up, victory is just around the corner. I was so glad that
I had decided to ignore my back pain and carry on. If
we persevere in the Lord, we always succeed.

In Dumfries I was privileged to preach to some
prisoners in the maximum security prison. They were
all serious offenders under the age of 21, and my
heart went out to them. To reach the chapel we went
through twelve doors, and I shuddered as each one
clanged shut behind me and was locked with a jangle
of keys. As a farmer who spends his time in the open
fields, I was beginning to feel claustrophobic.

Lindi and I visited that prison three times, and
each time we were thrilled to see a number of the
young inmates accept Jesus Christ as their personal
Lord and Saviour. Most of them were lost young men,
bored stiff by their aimless lives. One day I described
to them the magnificent African fish eagle, and told
them how they too could fly like an eagle, even in
prison, if they had the vision. My heart was warmed as
I watched those youngsters in their prison uniforms,
with their crew-cut hair exposing their youthful faces,
making a public confession of their faith.

The last time we went in there was about six weeks
into our journey, and we were feeling very homesick.

"I know I'll be home in three weeks, Lord, but it's so long to wait!" The Lord reminded me that some of these young men were in jail for long sentences: it would be far longer before they saw their homes again. I repented of my selfishness.

We were blessed with meeting some wonderful people, and their generosity overwhelmed us. They offered us hospitality in houses, mansions, farms and fishermen's cottages; they fed us and welcomed us and sent us on our way. In Dornach, in the far north of Scotland, a brother in Christ called Douglas Reid handed me a small parcel. Inside was a beautiful silver pin shaped like a sword, with a wide handle and a double-edged blade. The note he had written said: "Always keep preaching the gospel with no compromise, cutting through bone and marrow with God's holy word." In another town a woman was saved by the Lord from her life of prostitution, and she gave me a wooden spoon bearing the words, "Called with a holy calling".

The most amazing gift of all came towards the end of our time in Scotland. We were invited to preach at a church in Peterhead, once one of the largest fishing ports in Europe, and it was a wonderful meeting. I preached the gospel message and made the altar call, and afterwards I was praying with the sick when I saw a middle-aged man walking up the aisle towards me.

"Laddie," he said, "how long are ye going to be here for?"

"About another half-hour," I replied.

"Don't go away," he said quietly. "Wait here for me." I had just finished the prayer time when he came back, thrusting a parcel of clothes into my arms. "This is for you," he said. I could hardly believe my eyes. Not only was there a kilt, but also a dress jacket, belt, sporran and kilt pin. His name was Robert Buchan and of course it was a genuine Buchan tartan.

I was so stunned that I said the first thing that came into my head.

"How much do I owe you?"

He glared at me. "You don't understand, laddie," he said. "The Lord told me to give this to you."

It was amazing – of all the men in Scotland, Robert Buchan was identical to me in build, and his kilt fitted me perfectly. I promised him that I would wear it to preach whenever the opportunity arose.

We said our farewells to Scotland with love in our hearts, hoping that one day we would be able to return. Then we joyfully turned our faces for home.

When we arrived at Jan Smuts Airport, Johannesburg, the whole family was there to greet us. I walked through the airport with Lindi at my side, rejoicing in the new closeness we had developed after nine weeks together, father and daughter. During that time I had got to know her properly as an adult, a strong young woman who loved God, and I was so proud of her.

Andrew, strong and sturdy as ever, had come from university to be with us. He was studying agriculture and I knew that one day he would make a fine farmer. Beside him stood Robyn, of all my children the one who reminds me most of Jill. She has a gift for praise and worship, and a great love for children, especially those with disabilities.

Fergus, in his teens, seemed to have grown since I last saw him! He reminds me of my dad – a quiet, strong character with a natural ability with animals. I was sure Fergus would be the stockman of the family. Like all the children, he came to know the Lord at a young age. When he was just a little boy he brought me a scripture that he was sure had a special meaning for me. It was 1 Corinthians 1:17: "For Christ did not send me to baptise, but to preach the gospel – not with words of human wisdom, lest the cross of Christ be emptied of its power." It was a profound encouragement to me, as I was painfully aware of my lack of "human wisdom".

Lastly there was little Jilly, beaming from ear to ear as she caught sight of us entering the arrivals area. She is the bouncing ball of the family, a cheerful optimist – the family say she takes after her dad. They also say she can wrap me round her little finger!

I stood there in the kilt that God had sent me, and thanked him for the love of my family. They had driven 250 miles to meet us, and what a reunion we had! I hugged Jill and praised God for a beautiful wife who had stood faithfully by my side, encouraging me with her wise counsel and support, loving, comforting and praying for me every day.

It was wonderful to be back, and when we drove in through the gate to Shalom, my heart was filled with peace. I was at home where I belonged, with my family all around me, and work to do for the Lord. What more could a man want?

However, when I had been at home a few days I began to feel restless and discontented. Perhaps I was tired after nine weeks of travelling, but home just didn't feel the same, somehow. We had a traditional kind of marriage: I ran the farm and handled the finances; Jill looked after the home and the children. I loved to farm; she loved to sew and paint and tend the garden. I was the talker and the evangelist; Jill was the quiet one, the intercessor. We had always complemented each other, and worked together smoothly and easily as the team God designed us to be. Now something was different.

While I was away, Jill had learned to hold things together at the home base. She was signing cheques, making decisions and fixing all the things I would normally do when I was at home. Out on the farm, Steyn was doing an excellent job, planning and organising the workforce and working his heart out. The farm was in good order and the fields were being prepared for planting in the spring. Of course I was pleased – but deep down, I felt as if something had been taken from me. What was my role now?

Even my little Staffordshire terrier, Scruffy, didn't recognise me. Before I went to Scotland, Scruffy would only travel with me in my bakkie and no one else. She followed me everywhere, always on my heels when I walked around the garden or out in the fields. Now she walked straight past me and sat at the feet of Glenn, our adopted son. "See, even the dog doesn't need you," whispered a familiar voice in my ear. That hurt. What was the matter with me?

The trouble was that I felt redundant in the very place where I had built my life. I came back from Scotland to find the home being managed very capably by Jill, and the farm being managed efficiently by Steyn. It was exactly what I had planned and hoped for, but I hadn't predicted that it would make me feel completely worthless.

I had had an effective ministry in Scotland, and I knew I could do so in South Africa: already a full programme of meetings and campaigns had been planned for my return. Yet the place that was closest to my heart, Shalom, seemed to be slipping away from me. We had been farming here for close on 30 years, and now Jesus had sent another brother to continue the farming so that I could do the Lord's work and bring in that harvest of souls he had promised me. Shalom now belonged to Jesus, and it would never be mine again. At the same time my lovely wife had picked up my share of the burden of our home life and was carrying it effortlessly – another thing I didn't need to worry about.

These were great blessings. So why was I so depressed? It was one of the lowest periods of my Christian life. I don't think there is any worse situation for a person to be in than to feel totally useless and of no benefit to anyone. A feeling of worthlessness like that comes straight from the pit of hell, and the devil never misses the chance to discourage us. I was being made to recognise, all over again, just what I had given up for the sake of the gospel. I was being made to count the cost of my covenant vow to God. I had to deal with my feelings of loss, and remind myself that everything I had was a gift from God; I was only returning it to him. I bowed before him again.

"Lord, I accept that I may have no role at Shalom now. It's a small price to pay for the privilege of preaching the gospel."

At once the peace of the Lord filled my soul, and the restlessness left me. As soon as I surrendered to God's will for my life, my joy came back. How could I have doubted? I knew that God had my life safe in his hand, and that my path was planned: I was filled with energy and a new enthusiasm for my calling as a preacher.

I received afresh the vision of what Shalom could be: a place where the Holy Spirit could move freely, a place of prayer and a refuge for the needy. It wasn't just the source of our funding but also a place where God's work was done, in the chapel and the houses and the people who came to seek sanctuary with us. Combining the two sides of my life – farming and preaching the gospel – it would always be at the heart of my ministry.

I felt as though, at the moment of renouncing my ownership of Shalom, giving it over wholly to the Lord, it had been given back to me. "For whoever wants to save his life will lose it, but whoever loses his life for me and for the gospel will save it" (Mark 8:35). We serve a generous God.

9
Shalom's Children

*O*nce again, bowing in obedience to God led to a significant move forward in our ministry. The community at Shalom had already touched many lives, and it was about to touch many more.

Mike Henderson wasn't a Christian, but he knew about Shalom: he worked for the Lion Match Company, whose land bordered ours. In October 1994 his only son Shaun was killed in a hit-and-run accident, and Mike and his wife Colleen were devastated. Shortly afterwards Mike came to see me.

"Angus, there's something I want to do," he said. "I want to erect a cross in memory of Shaun, and I want it to be here at Shalom."

When I asked him why, he told me that the Lord had given him a vision of a giant white cross, twelve metres high, standing beside our chapel – and this was an unbeliever speaking! We were glad to agree, and when the cross was erected, Shaun's ashes were scattered beneath it in a simple ceremony.

Mike and Colleen accepted the Lord as their Saviour in December the same year, and some months later Mike received a miraculous healing.

"I suffer from back problems," he told us at our weekly Bible study, "and I go to a chiropractor in Pietermaritzburg every month. I would love to be free of my back pain."

He was sitting in a chair with his legs stretched in front of him. Jill and two other friends placed their hands on him while I anointed him with oil and prayed the prayer of faith. Suddenly, in front of our eyes, his right leg seemed to stretch out. We watched in awe as it grew. The next day Mike went back to the chiropractor and asked him for a thorough examination. He was amazed at the improvement in Mike's condition. "God did a miracle," Mike said. "My life has been changed for ever."

The cross Mike and Colleen erected is illuminated at night: as the sun goes down, the lights come on. The local airstrip uses it as a landmark for planes coming in to land. It is visible for miles in the dark as it bears testimony to the Lord Jesus Christ and the power of the gospel. I remember coming home late one evening and seeing Mike's pickup parked by the side of the dirt road. As I drove by I saw Mike sitting inside, alone, looking up at the cross on the hill, and doubtless thinking of his dear son Shaun, who is safe in the precious arms of Jesus.

Just as that cross has become a landmark in the area, so Shalom was becoming a landmark in people's lives, whether they came for a visit or stayed to live and work alongside us. One of the keynote Bible verses that means a lot to us is from James: "Religion that God our Father accepts as pure and faultless is this: to look after orphans and widows in their distress and to keep oneself from being polluted by the world" (James 1:27). This idea is incorporated in our vision for Shalom, which is written up clearly on the wall of the chapel for the community and the fellowship to see. It is very simple and has three points:

• The Great Commission, preaching the gospel to the lost;
• To take care of the widows and the orphans;
• To equip the saints for the work of the Lord.

Among the many people who came to help us at Shalom were Jimmy Mathieson and his wife Moyra. Jimmy was like a father to me. Every morning after my dad died Jimmy would come and have a cup of coffee with me, and every day he would share something he had learned from the Bible and say something of real relevance to my life. I can still hear him: "You're working too hard, Angus." "You must spend more time with your family." "You're on the road too much." After he died his widow, Moyra, stayed on at Shalom. She moved into a little cottage on the farm.

Not long afterwards I had the privilege of attending a very special party. Peggy O'Neill, a widow who was closely involved with our work, had invited me to her 70th birthday party. There, in the middle of the celebrations, she stood up in front of her entire family and announced that she was going into full-time work for Jesus!

"I'm going to join Angus and Jill at Shalom Ministries as an intercessor."

That was over ten years ago, and Peggy is still with

Angus Buchan, played by Frank Rautenbach, rejoices as rain douses a runaway fire on his farm.

Simeon Bhengu, played by Hamilton Dhlamini, builds the roof of his hut on Shalom Farm.

Jill Buchan, played by Jeanne Wilhelm, looks out from the window of their farm in Zambia.

Simeon and Angus harvest the first potato from the miracle harvest.

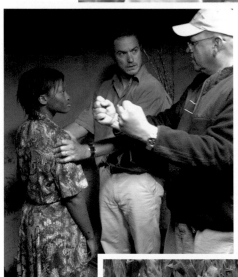

Regardt van den Bergh directs Frank and Ayanda in a scene where Angus prays for a woman to be raised from the dead.

Frans Cronje (Producer), Frank Rautenbach (Lead actor) and Regardt van den Bergh (Director) on the set of Shalom Farm.

Angus tells his friend Koos about his conversion to Christianity, over a beer in the local pub.

Angus desperately tries to stop a runaway fire from spreading onto neighbouring farms.

Frank Rautenbach stands in the middle of the set while shooting the runaway fire.

Isaiah, played by Sam Ximba, who is a local Greytown pastor in real life, chats with Simeon at the Zulu compound.

Kevin O'Reilly, 1st Assistant Director, sprays Frank with water between takes – he's just come in out of a rainstorm.

Cameraman Lee Doig on the crane above Ewie Cronje, who plays Alistair.

Simeon and some of the farm workers fight to put out the runaway fire on Angus's farm.

Regardt van den Bergh in typical pose, directing one of the fire scenes.

Angus & Simeon pray just before digging up the potatoes.

Frans Cronje, Regardt van den Bergh, Angus Buchan and Ewie Cronje (Frans' father) chat on the set of *Faith Like Potatoe*s on Shalom Farm.

Fergus Buchan, played by Sean Cameron Michael, dreams of his son Alistair, played by Ewie Cronje.

Angus brings tea to his wife, Jill, in bed at home, on the Shalom Farm set.

A conversation between Angus and Steyn, played by Anton Treurnicht, being shot in front of the Shalom Farmhouse set.

Angus screams as he realises the extent of Alistair's injuries

Frank comforts Ewie after a long and emotional scene.

Jeanne waits to shoot a scene in the Methodist Church, Greytown, with Christopher Bartels who plays the Buchan's oldest son, Andy.

Frank Rautenbach, Jeanne Wilhelm, Jill & Angus Buchan, photographed in Angus & Jill's home on Shalom Farm, the same one they built when they arrived in Greytown.

Frank & Jeanne waiting to do a scene, on the set of the Shalom farmhouse. Frank is wearing the Buchan tartan kilt Angus was given in Scotland.

us, living in a little cottage next door to Moyra. The pair of them pray for us without ceasing. We support and care for our widows, but they do far more for us: they are real prayer warriors, and uphold everything we do. Their intercessions are a source of strength and guidance as we seek God's will for ways to fulfil the Shalom vision. A vital part of that is our care for Shalom's children.

In the early 1990s we were becoming aware of a significant problem: HIV/AIDS was ravaging South Africa, and our area, KwaZulu-Natal, was one of the worst affected. (By 2000, around 36 per cent of the population was recorded as infected.) This terrible disease affects the young adults who are sexually active, who are also the generation of working age. Consequently there are thousands of families living in the deepest poverty, with no adult breadwinners or carers left alive. Some of these families are headed by a grandparent or older sibling, who struggles to feed and care for several young children, but there are also many orphaned children who have no one to look after them.

As I travelled around our area, the plight of these abandoned children wrung my heart. Those whose parents had died of AIDS were often HIV-positive themselves. Often they were living in terrible conditions, in broken-down hovels with their clothing in tatters. Many were close to starvation. How could we live in the middle of such plenty when God's children were going hungry only a few miles away?

My heart broke for them and I wanted to do something practical to help.

"What shall I do, Lord? Find foster-parents? Give money? Give food?"

I sensed the quiet voice of the Spirit of God.

"Build a children's home at Shalom, Angus, and take care of them yourself."

It was a venture of faith: we knew nothing about how to go about such a task. We were blessed by having Tommy Blackbourne as a helper. He is a big man in every sense of the word, with a warm smile and broad Scots accent. He was born in a tough area of Glasgow – where he came from, he said, it was so dangerous that even the dogs walked around in pairs! He not only helped us with the building work, but also took care of all the legal details and endless papers that had to be completed for the Department of Welfare.

We decided to call our children's home *Beth Hatlaim*, which is Hebrew for "The House of the Lambs", and to build it on a high spot on the farm, looking out over the forests. We had no idea where the building materials would come from, but a miraculous thing happened. I happened to hear that the local high school in Greytown wanted to get rid of some old prefabricated buildings they had been using as classrooms. I approached the headmaster, and he was happy to donate them to us, if we would undertake to remove them from the site. Tommy and I and a few Zulu workmen took the truck into town and spent several days dismantling the buildings, putting the walls, roofs and wooden floors into the truck and hauling them back to the farm.

It was hard work but we were happy to do it: God

loves to open doors for us when we walk in faith. Some people would say that such an event was a coincidence, but we thought differently. How many coincidences do you need to see before you accept that there is such a thing as a "God-incidence"?

Back at the farm we threw out all the rubbish and scrubbed every bit of the buildings before we re-erected them. We had to pay special attention to cleanliness and hygiene, as many of our children would be HIV-positive, which makes them especially vulnerable to infection. The three buildings provided space for two dormitories – one each for the boys and the girls – and a nursery for the babies. Then we started building the kitchen, bathrooms and dining room. Our children's home was beginning to take shape.

The day we finished building we heard about another school hostel that was closing down, and we were able to make a successful bid for all their beds and wardrobes. Believers in Scotland heard about our plans and sent us a seven-metre ship's container packed with prams, cots, clothing, bicycles and a host of other items. The Rotary Club donated a washing machine and tumble drier. Someone else appeared with a huge tray of cutlery. God provided for that home in the most amazing ways.

There is a spring in the valley, so we were able to pump water into a collecting tank, from where it could be gravity-fed into the houses. When we needed hot water for bathing or washing we heated it in 44-gallon drums over a wood fire.

From the start we had a big playroom where all the

children could congregate in the evenings; it was especially useful when it was cold, as it could be heated easily. We also hoed out all the scrub in the area and planted trees and lawns, so that it would be a pleasant place for the children to run around outside. Then we built the biggest-ever "jungle gym" with climbing frames and rope swings, and it proved to be a big hit with the children.

However much we built and planted and painted, however, the home would be nothing without the right people to care for the children.

"We need someone to run with this vision, Lord," we prayed. "Please send us the right person."

God sent us Choekie Rawlins. Her husband had been killed in an accident at work, and she came to us as a young widow with three small children of her own. She is a state registered nurse, so she was the ideal person to care for our little ones, and she did a marvellous work with them in the time she was with us. The Lord also raised up a willing staff to help care for the children round the clock in shifts. Some are women from the local community; others are full-time care workers who have come from the worlds of commerce and industry because they have caught the vision.

For months, as we worked on the buildings, we had been enquiring about the possibility of taking in children, but we ran into all kinds of bureaucracy. The very day we completed building in faith, our first orphan arrived. The Lord started sending us the babies of HIV/AIDS victims, children who had been born in the local hospital and abandoned there. Most of them had never been outside the hospital ward, and they were terrified of going outside and playing on the grass. It's a great joy to me now to see them playing happily in the sun. We work closely with the local social workers and co-operate with the local authorities, who pay us a meagre stipend each month for food and clothing for each child we adopt. It doesn't come anywhere close to the real cost of caring for these children, so once again we are living by faith, and trusting the Lord for the rest.

We started with ten children, many of whom were suffering from HIV/AIDS, and needed intensive care. We nursed them and we prayed for them, because our God is a healing God: "Jesus Christ is the same yesterday and today and for ever" (Hebrews 13:8). We saw his healing in our children, as they slowly gained weight and stopped coughing so much, their sores faded and their skin grew smooth and healthy. They thrive on the Shalom regime of good food, a regular routine, discipline and lots of love.

Over the years we have lost nine infants, usually in the early weeks. Every time we lose a baby because of AIDS, my heart breaks. That's the sad side of this ministry of caring for abandoned babies, but we are trusting the Lord for them. I remember little Thoko, just seven years old, who died of AIDS. He was a tiny little boy, just skin and bone, but he loved coming for rides with me on my horse. Whenever he saw me he would stick up his thumb in victory. Just before he died he told me a secret. "Jesus is coming for me on his white horse," he said. It comforts my heart that these precious little ones hear the gospel from the first day they arrive here. The teaching of the Bible is shared with them every day, and they are cared for in body, mind and spirit.

These desperately sick children are the ones whom no one else wants, and they have no relatives or carers in the local community. Occasionally there is so little known about them that we have had to check their teeth to make a guess at their ages; sometimes we have even had to give them a name. Now they are part of our family, and we are very proud of them. For several years my youngest daughter Jilly, who is a nurse, ran the children's home. Now she is married and lives with her husband Greg on his farm on the other side of Greytown, but she remains responsible for the children's health. She travels in three or four times a week to check on them. They all love her dearly, and sometimes one or two go home with her for a visit.

As our babies grew up we realised that we needed to build a school for them, so a little pre-school was established, and later we added a junior school. From there they move on to Halalisani School on a neighbouring farm. This school serves the whole local area, and Jill and I are the managers. It has 200 pupils, including some children from Shalom (others go to the high school in Greytown). All our teachers are Christians, and their salaries are subsidised by the government, but each farm school is only allowed a set number of teachers. We feel we need more than that minimum number, so the rest are paid for out of our own pockets. We are very proud of the way the school has developed: this year it won the prize for the best-presented rural school in KwaZulu-Natal.

There is only one white person in the school – my daughter Robyn, who is a "higher grade" English teacher. She divides her time between the children's home (where she has taken over some of Jilly's work) and the school, where she teaches part-time. It was important that however capable and well-qualified Robyn was, a white person should not be at the head of our school: in a country where class distinction and racism are still rampant, actions always speak louder than words. Our Zulu headmistress, Mrs Rita Nxumalo, is a beautiful Christian woman who regards Robyn as one of her own children.

It's very good for our children to leave the farm to go to school. Sometimes children who live in orphanages can be cut off from the rest of the world, but ours go off to school and mix with the children from all the other farms in the area. They bring their friends home to play and have tea or to sleep over just like any other kids, and they visit their friends' homes in the same way. They go to church on the farm and some of their friends' parents come to our chapel too, so there is constant interaction with the local community.

Many of our orphans are very bright and talented. One boy, Khumbulani Sithole, has always been a great athlete. He has been admitted to Clifton, the preparatory school for Michaelhouse (the South African equivalent of Eton) on a full bursary, which is a wonderful opportunity for him. He has been chosen to represent the province of Natal in the under-twelve rugby team.

When I go to the open days at the public school (which is frightfully English, I have to say), I'm the only father who has white hair, but I'm still his dad and he's happy to see me there. Recently he said to me, "When I'm big I'm going to change my name – to Khumbulani Buchan." What an honour.

We have another young man who is an excellent horseman and who is playing competitive sport on horseback; another is a good musician, but more importantly these youngsters love the Lord Jesus Christ and are serving him. This didn't happen overnight. It has taken years and years of patient prayer and guidance, trusting in Jesus for his care for these young people.

My relationship as a "father in the Lord" with these children is very precious to me. One day I was driving down the farm track in the pickup, with two of the little boys, aged about four or five, sitting beside me. One of them turned to me conversationally and said, "*Baba*, don't worry. When you get old one day, you'll be sitting here where we are, and we'll be driving you around!" So I don't need to worry about a pension – I'm investing in things that last for ever.

It's the younger children who call me *Baba* – as they get older, I become "Dad". When I attend the prize-giving at their schools I sit there with my arms folded and my chest sticking out, barely able to contain my pride as our children win prizes: the most improved student, the best sportsman of the year, the most advanced academically.

"Look, Dad, what I've got!" They bring me their certificates and I stick my chest out even further, but I give all the glory to God. He is so faithful and gracious.

One day a friend came to visit, and as we sat

together over a cup of coffee, we talked about the ministry at Shalom. He said that what impressed him most was not the big campaigns or the media interviews, but the family atmosphere he senses on the farm. Seeing our children's home still going strong after all these years, and watching our children growing into confident, lovely young men and women is what touches him most.

One of our boys plays polocrosse with my son Fergus – they both love the tough, demanding nature of this very active contact sport, and the camaraderie between the two of them is obvious. My friend said that he was at one of the sports practices when he saw some of the other players teasing Fergus.

"Is this your brother, then?" they asked.

Fergus didn't hesitate. He flung his arm round his friend's shoulders and said, "Of course he is." That touched my friend more than any sermon he had heard from me.

Not all our children's stories end happily. When Robyn was working at a school for underprivileged children in Pietermaritzburg she met two children who were shockingly neglected. The boy was about four years old and his sister six. They came to school unwashed, with their clothes torn and grubby; their eyes were sunken and dull and they were clearly not properly fed. Robyn used to come home and tell us how concerned she was for their welfare. Their mother worked the streets and Robyn guessed that they were often left alone at home.

She asked us to pray about taking these two waifs into our own home, but Jill and I hesitated. Our own family had grown up and were leaving home, and we weren't sure we wanted to take in two more small children at this stage of our lives.

"But we can't just leave them there!" cried Robyn.

In the end she brought them home to us, and we fostered them for around four years. In that time they blossomed. Liam grew more confident, and Mary grew into a lovely little girl, trusting and happy. Sadly, their mother took advantage of the situation. She pocketed her monthly allowance from the government for the two children, without telling the authorities that they were no longer living with her. Then she decided that she wanted them to come home, and they had to go back to her. It broke their hearts to leave the farm, and Liam especially was miserable at leaving Fergie, whom he idolised as a big brother. All we could do was pray for them, and hope that their years of security and care with us would bear fruit in their lives later on.

Meanwhile the orphanage goes on growing. We have somewhere in the region of half a million AIDS orphans in our province of KwaZulu-Natal alone, and deep though my satisfaction is that we are caring for our children so well, the plight of all those other children tears at my heart.

"What can we do to help, Lord?" I asked, and I sensed that God wanted us to step out in faith once more.

"It's time to increase the size of the orphanage," he told me. "I want you to take in more children."

So we are making preparations to extend the orphanage from 24 to 180 children. We have built four cottages so far, each with six children and a housemother to look after them. It's a system that suits the children very well: they have bonded with their new "families" and the children are absolutely glowing with health and happiness. The houses are sturdily built out of concrete blocks, and each has a proper geyser for instant hot water. We are building a central dining room, a meeting hall and a clinic, and the old dormitories have been turned into a computer room and a family room with a big TV screen. Once again, as we complete the building of a new house, God sends us the children to live in them. We believe that our Father in heaven will provide everything we need, because the vision comes from him.

10
God of Miracles

While things were progressing at the farm, we were still running gospel campaigns, and we were excited at what the Lord was doing.

In 1993 I was invited to preach in Cedarville, a town not far from Greytown. The organising committee had enlisted the help of Mike Francis, a prominent businessman. Mike was not a Christian, though his wife, June, had been praying for him for 27 years: he was a hard-drinking, smoking, sports-loving man, and a good organiser. It was nothing for him to hire a jumbo jet to fly his friends to London to watch the Springboks play England. Mike didn't have time for God in his life – he was far too busy travelling, running his business and piloting his plane or his ski-boat.

When he was asked to set up our meetings, he was hesitant. Eventually he agreed to help, provided he could meet me first. He wasn't going to invite any of his friends to something that might turn out to be an embarrassment.

I was working at the cattle-dip when I saw a sleek Mercedes Benz drive up to the house. When Mike got out and introduced himself, I was very conscious that I was filthy and smelt terrible: I wasn't surprised when he refused my invitation for coffee!

"I'm on my way to Durban and I'm in a hurry," he said. "Just tell me exactly what you're intending to do in Cedarville."

"Do you want to hear my testimony?" I asked.

"No," he said flatly, "I just want you to get to the point." I felt I was losing ground rapidly. I told him how we ran a campaign, and added, "We believe that Jesus gives people a reason for living – there are so many people in what seem to be hopeless situations."

"OK," he said, "I'll be in touch", and with that he got into his car and drove off. I didn't think he was the slightest bit interested in what we were doing.

I was surprised to receive a fax from Mike the following morning, showing a handbill he had designed for the campaign. It seemed we had him on board after all. It was accompanied by very precise instructions: there were to be no guitars, no drums, and no preliminaries. He would bring a CD player for a single hymn, and then I would be given the opportunity to speak. I found out later that he had also told his wife that there were to be no altar calls, but – praise the Lord – he forgot to tell me that.

When we arrived at Cedarville Town Hall it was full, and many of Mike's friends were among the crowd. We sang the hymn and I took the microphone to share a very simple message. At the end, I gave my usual invitation.

"If you want to receive Jesus Christ as your Lord and Saviour, please stand up and come to the front," I said. I told them that if they were ashamed to stand up for Christ there in the hall, they would never be able to stand up for him outside it.

There was a moment of silence, then 26 men got up and walked up the aisle; the third man was Mike Francis. That night he went home and wept tears of joy and repentance in front of his wife. From the night of his conversion he gave up both smoking and drinking and never looked back, and today Mike and June are in full-time evangelistic work, travelling all over South Africa to preach the gospel. God has performed an incredible miracle in their lives.

When I see things like that happening, it builds up my faith in the Lord Jesus, who has the power to transform lives. Over the years I have learned to trust him to move in power, whether it is in turning the hearts of men to himself, or showing his sovereignty over the elements, even when it looks as though nothing can possibly happen. Our campaign among the stockmen of the Eastern Cape was one such occasion.

At our first meeting in Cathcart Town Hall a large number of people had made a commitment to Jesus as their Saviour. It was farming country and I could sense the worry among the farmers I met.

"We're having the worst drought for years," they said. "Things are serious – we've only had around seven millimetres of rain at any one time. It's nowhere near enough."

As we talked, I could feel the insistent prompting of the Holy Spirit: "Tell the farmers that rain is coming."

So I stepped out in faith.

"It's going to rain soon. In fact, the rain will come

before we leave you." It was a bold statement – we were due to leave in four days, and there was no sign of a break in the weather.

As we travelled round the towns and villages in the area, we repeated the message. "Rain is coming." Expectancy began to grow, but the sky continued blue and cloudless. The Lord was busy building our faith. We trusted that God would keep his promise.

Our final meeting was held in a sheep-shearing shed in a place called Croomie. We arrived an hour before the meeting and it was so hot that I went outside and sat down on a milking stool in the shade. The sweet smell of the hay mingled with cow manure suddenly made me feel deeply homesick for my own farm. I bowed my head in prayer.

"Lord," I said, "the people will be here in half an hour. We're going home tomorrow and it hasn't rained a drop."

Just then, out of the corner of my eye, I thought I saw a distant light on the horizon – had it been a flash of lightning? I turned my head, but it was gone. Cars were arriving, and across the fields I could see the farm workers beginning to walk towards the shed. I got up.

"Well, Lord Jesus, this is it. I love you and trust you. Even if it doesn't rain, even if I've made myself look foolish for you, I will still go on trusting you and preaching your gospel."

A large crowd had gathered, and the farmers had laid on a beautiful cold buffet supper for us. Once we had eaten and given thanks to the Lord, the meeting began with praise and worship. Ian sang a beautiful, reflective song and turned to me. I stepped forward. Before I could open my mouth to speak, I heard a gentle pattering sound. Rain was falling on the tin roof of the shed. I could hardly believe my ears.

"Do you hear that? It's rain! That's my Jesus! I told you it was going to rain!"

The louder I spoke, the heavier it rained. A clap of thunder echoed through the shed and the rain poured down. It went on all night, and 37 millimetres of rain fell. The farmers were overjoyed and many of them committed their lives to Jesus. It was an evening we would never forget.

The next morning we woke to the beautiful smell of freshly fallen rain on the earth, and we boarded our plane and made our way home rejoicing. Once again the devil had been defeated and Jesus had the victory.

Another spectacular time the Lord sent us rain in direct answer to prayer was in Nongoma, far in the north-east of the province. Our campaign was due to run for a week, and we travelled around in a bakkie, using a loudspeaker to invite people to attend our meetings. On the first day we drove 20 kilometres or so out of town and climbed a dirt track into the mountains of Zululand. We came across a group of the local headmen seated in the shade of a large tree, having a meeting called *indaba sibantu*, discussing all the business of the district. If we could tell them about our campaign, we might make contact with all the people of their villages.

Duduzo, my guide, approached them and explained why we were in the area, and they agreed to allow me to come and address them. I came forward and sat down on one of the small stools they had put out for us.

"We have come here to preach the gospel of Jesus Christ," I said. I reminded them of the power of our Lord, and talked about the signs and wonders that the Bible promises will take place wherever the gospel is preached.

"May I pray with you before we leave?" I asked.

They agreed, and one of the elders had a request.

"We have had no rain here for a whole year," he said. "Not a single drop. We can grow nothing without rain. Will you pray about that?"

We closed our eyes and began to pray, and the Lord led me to say a very specific prayer.

"Lord, please send rain today!"

It was a bold prayer: why should today be any different from any other?

We went back to our pickup and drove back to town; our meetings began that evening. As we were walking to the hall, the rain started coming down. It rained that night, and all the next day. In fact, it rained every single day that we were there, and somewhere out there in the hills a group of headmen knew that our Lord answers prayer.

On the Wednesday I preached about the story of the prodigal son. Many of the Zulu people had never heard the Bible, and the Lord prompted me to localise the story to help them understand.

I told them that a young man by the name of Sipho Bengu was looking after his father's farm and cattle. As the Zulu's wealth depends on the ownership of cattle, it is an honourable thing to be able to look after them.

"So Sipho looked after his father's wealth, milking the cattle early in the morning, and working in the fields all day. One day a friend of his, who had gone off to the gold mines in Johannesburg, came home for a spot of leave. His name was Joe Mthethwa. Joe came down the road wearing his smart new trousers and shiny new shoes. His hair was slicked back with gel and he had a portable radio on his shoulder. He looked as if the world was his oyster.

"That night Sipho went to his father and asked him for his inheritance, because he was sick of working on the farm and he wanted to go to Johannesburg with Joe. His father reluctantly sold two of the oxen, gave Sipho the money, and said, 'God bless you.'

"Sipho set off for Johannesburg. When he arrived at the station he was set upon by robbers, who stole all his money. He tried to get a job, but he couldn't find one – the city was full of boys from the country, looking for work. He began eating scraps. He walked along railway tracks to pick up fallen bits of sugarcane to try to keep his hunger at bay.

"After a while he thought, 'I'm worse off than my father's cattle. I'll go back to my father's house and ask his forgiveness.' The Holy Spirit must have given him strength, because he walked all the way home.

"When he saw his home, he was ashamed of what he had done. He thought he would wait until nightfall before he went in. But his father was so excited to see him that he took his best robe and put it on Sipho, and slaughtered an ox for a feast. He said, 'My son was lost, but now he is found.' And he received him back into the family with joy."

My audience listened intently. Two days later a young Zulu man came to see me. He looked at me with tears in his eyes.

"That was exactly what happened to me when I was twelve years old. I also came back late at night, but it was my grandmother who was waiting for me, not my father."

He said that he had repented and received God's forgiveness, and asked me for a copy of the audiotape we always make of meetings, so he could keep listening to "his" story. As he was leaving he turned back to me.

"By the way," he said, "my name is Sipho."

The greatest compliment I have ever received came from a Zulu preacher in Magaliesberg. He said, "That's not a white man. It's a black man with a white man's skin." He meant that my years of working shoulder to shoulder with my Zulu friends had given me an understanding of their way of thinking, and I had even picked up Zulu mannerisms in my speech. I have a great love for the Zulu people, so I was delighted when the Lord told me to plan a crusade in Ulundi, the Zulu capital.

I had a strong desire to meet the king of the Zulus, King Goodwill Zwelithini, and ask his blessing for the campaign, but I didn't think it would be possible. How easy would it be for an English farmer to drop in and have a chat with the queen of England? By a series of contacts organised by the Lord, against all probability, I was granted an audience with the king.

I was very nervous, as I had no idea of the protocol for meeting such a person, the king of a nation of over eight million people. When I arrived at the gates of the palace, there were crowds of people in traditional Zulu dress, hoping to get a glimpse of their monarch. They were shouting, "*Bayete, Nkosi* (We salute you, O king)."

Armed soldiers led us into the building, taking off their shoes as they entered. Inside the inner chamber, they got on their knees and crawled towards the king. I was led to a chair, very aware of the respect in which the king is held.

When I was invited to speak, I got to my feet and testified to the miracle-working power of Jesus Christ. I spoke in Zulu, the king's language, and everybody listened with rapt attention. At the back of my mind I could hear the Holy Spirit saying to me, "You are an ambassador of the Lord Jesus Christ, the King of Kings. You need fear no one except God."

I shared with the king the details of our coming crusade in Ulundi and asked his blessing. When we left – at the end of a long day in which we were royally entertained – the king himself came to shake our hands and bid us goodbye.

"Please keep praying for me," he said. "Without the power of God I cannot rule this nation."

The subsequent campaign in Ulundi was conducted in difficult conditions – we camped in caravans with no water supply – but it was greatly blessed. It was moving to see the Zulu people so hungry for the things of God and it made us more reliant on the Lord than ever.

The meetings were vibrant with the presence of God. Hundreds responded each night and came forward to receive Jesus as their Saviour, and many more came for prayer and healing. The Zulu people have tremendous faith, and we were awed by the miracles taking place all around us, as people were healed and delivered from smoking and drug and alcohol abuse.

April 1994 was a historic date for South Africa: the first democratic elections were held. For the first time ever, black people were allowed to vote alongside white people for the government of their choice. Everyone went from Shalom farm to Sevenoaks village, where the polling booth was set up, and we stood in line together. It was a wonderful day. However, we all knew that this was only the first step on a long road for our country. Nothing was going to change overnight. In many ways, the famous "new South Africa" was a change in name only; the old resentments still festered, and the old injustices would take a long time to be undone. We rejoiced at Shalom because among us we knew true reconciliation in Christ, since "there is neither Jew nor Greek, slave nor free, male nor female, for you are all one in Christ Jesus" (Galatians 3:28). We worked together side by side, and we trusted each other as brothers and sisters in Christ. That was not the case in many other places, where anger flared up into violence, and people walked in fear.

At that time KwaZulu-Natal was in terrible turmoil, and a tremendous burden for the farmers of the area filled my heart. Every day we heard of violence or another murder, and it seemed as if the farmers in the Natal Midlands were being specially targeted. Some of the killings occurred in the course of a theft, others were political, or resulted from vendettas between employers and workers. Many were racially motivated. The days of apartheid were over, but in many people's eyes the white farmers (who were usually the main employers in the area) were inextricably linked with the old days of racism and oppression. Some of my personal friends had been robbed or burgled; several had been killed. We were on the edge of anarchy.

By December 1996 we had conducted 22 major campaigns across the eastern part of South Africa, and I was waiting for the Lord to tell me where we should go next. I had never become confident of doing anything in my own strength – I am still the same blunt farmer as I ever was – but I had faith that if I opened myself to God he would use me to speak to his children.

The Spirit of God impressed on my heart that the future of KwaZulu-Natal – and indeed the whole country – lies in the hands of its people. "If my people, who are called by my name, will humble themselves and pray and seek my face and turn from their wicked ways, then will I hear from heaven and will forgive their sin and will heal their land" (2 Chronicles 7:14).

As I waited for the Lord to guide me I remembered that the Boers – the farmers of old – were a God-fearing people. In the days when they first settled in South Africa and began to farm here they used to spend whole weekends together, worshipping God. They would gather from their distant farms on the Saturday, and place their wagons around the church and camp there. They would meet and have fellowship together, taking the opportunity for socialising and meeting their friends. On the Sunday they would hold their communion service in the morning before hitching their teams of oxen and setting off for home.

My vision was to see the farmers of KwaZulu-Natal meeting again, but this time as a witness for peace in the area. I knew I would need a huge venue for such an event, and the ideal place came into my head. The King's Park Stadium in Durban was at that time the biggest rugby stadium in the world. I didn't know how I was going to fill it, and I didn't know how I was going to finance it, but that was the place we had to be.

God worked many miracles for us in the preparation for the King's Park Peace Gathering, miracles of financial provision and Christian support, and in time everything came together as he had shown me. The farmers of the area caught my vision and promised that they would be there. They would camp around the stadium with their workers, a sign of our unity in Christ. We were out to do battle against sin, violence and Christian lethargy, not with guns and ammunition but with the weapons of spiritual warfare.

Everywhere we went, in churches and town halls and villages, we asked people to join us. "If you are tired of the violence," we told them, "be there! Come and call on the Lord in repentance with the farmers. Only God can heal our land. Let's confess Jesus Christ as Lord of KwaZulu-Natal."

The event took place one weekend in September 1997, and we were amazed at the numbers of people who came. Farmers and their workers from right across the province made their way to the stadium

and set up their caravans and tents. We had all our
workers from Shalom farm sleeping with us in one
big tent; we killed two sheep and made a huge stew
which we shared. Youth groups arrived en masse;
churches of all denominations were there. Around
15,000 people braved the cold, wet weather to hear
from God.

I could feel the Holy Spirit moving in that place as
Ian led the singing in Zulu and English. As we worshipped together, we were aware of the Lord drawing
us together in spirit.

"Without Jesus, the Prince of Peace," I told the people, "there will be no peace in our land. We've come
together to ask God to give us one more chance. We've
come to say, 'Lord, we are prepared to repent so that
we can save our province and our nation.'

"Someone once said that it was not the violence of
the few that scared him, so much as the silence of the
many. How dare we sit in front of our televisions and
criticise the government and the laws of the land,
while we are doing nothing ourselves?

"It's time for Christians to get moving. Revival is
going to come, but it's going to come through ordinary people like you and me. It's time to stop complaining and get involved."

When I gave the altar call that night, literally thousands and thousands of people stood up – men,
women and children, black and white, rich and poor –
and called on the name of the Lord in a spirit of deep
repentance. I was awed at the spirit of reconciliation
that was among them.

We had been asked not to let people come onto the

rugby field, as a big game was scheduled the following weekend, so we had to bring them in groups to a small area cordoned off in front of the platform. I have never prayed for so many people individually as I did that night. Hundreds of people were standing before me, with needs ranging from depression to cancer. One young girl got out of her wheelchair and started walking for the first time in her life. Others were healed of back pain. One testified that his eyes had been healed and he could see better without his glasses than with them! We ministered to the sick until 11.30 that night.

The next day we were back, and the amazing scenes were repeated, and even more people came. We had many dignitaries – mayors and provincial leaders – all sharing the same vision. Dr Mangosuthu Buthelezi, the Inkatha Freedom Party leader, arrived by helicopter; Jacob Zuma, the ANC (African National Congress) leader was sitting in the stands with his Bible open on his lap. Once again we preached the Lordship of Christ and his message of peace, and once again hundreds came forward for prayer. Afterwards Dr Buthelezi wrote me a letter.

"It was a great privilege to participate in the Peace Gathering at King's Park," he said. "It was so strengthening to be in the company of so many believers. I went home spiritually replenished."

It was a joy to us, too, and we believed we had seen a ray of light in the darkness that affected so many of our towns. A year later the Lord directed my thoughts to another needy place: Richmond, a very small town nestled in the beautiful green hills of the Natal Midlands.

On the edge of Richmond there is a township, set up in the days of apartheid when black people were not allowed to live in the "whites-only" areas of town. The black people would travel into the town each day to work, often in the smart, well-equipped homes of white people, and then go home at night to their own houses without heating, power or running water. The township was a place of poverty, and the new South African democracy had not performed any overnight miracles for its people. Many of them were poor, unemployed and angry, and there was a lot of violence. People were dying every day, and my heart went out to them. I longed to take the gospel there. As my concern for the Zulu settlement grew, I extended my quiet time with God: I needed his guidance. I waited on the Lord in prayer, and he began to instruct me about Richmond.

The township is divided into two parts, Indaleni and Magoda. There had been a terrible bloodbath in the area over the years as two rival political parties fought each other for supremacy. In the old days Zulu fighting was restricted to the men, but now women and children were being killed as the traditional knobkerry (a wooden club) gave way to the AK47 (a Russian-made automatic rifle).

God's instruction was clear. "Put a huge tent right in the middle of the township. Place it in the no-man's-land between the two factions and watch what I will do."

I love a challenge and I started getting excited. This was such a bad trouble spot that there were more army and police personnel than residents: police patrolled the area with horses, motor bikes, armoured cars and helicopters. It was costing the country millions of Rand.

"Over 500 people have already lost their lives there, Lord," I said. "It's the exact place where the tent should go."

On 4 November 1998 we erected a massive 5,000-seat tent on the marshland separating the two communities. A crowd of people watched silently as we worked, and we could feel their suspicion. Who was this white man? How long would he stay? In the eyes of many I was already a dead man. I had taken only a very small team with me: it was a dangerous mission and I only wanted people who knew they had been called by God.

We were not afraid, though we often felt the spirit of evil that covered the area, especially at night. There was just a piece of canvas between us and the chaos outside. Hungry dogs scavenged around the camp, foraging in the rubbish bins and fighting over scraps. In the streets nearby we could hear screams and gunshots. We prayed for the Lord's protection, and received it. No one was harmed in the whole three weeks; not even one of our banners was torn down.

When I went outside that first morning I was amazed: I had never seen such a military presence in my life. Soldiers and police were everywhere, helicopters buzzed overhead, and armoured cars were in position on every hilltop. This was definitely a war zone.

"We can't come out after dark," people told us. "It's much too dangerous. You'll have to preach in the afternoon."

So we started the meeting at four o'clock that afternoon. At first just a trickle of people arrived, mainly women and children, but they were followed by the men, and eventually there were hundreds of people there. I concentrated on preaching the word of God straight out of the Bible. Then we prayed for the sick and God did some amazing miracles of healing. When we made the altar call, many people gave their lives to the Lord.

As the sun went down I spoke to the crowd in the tent. "It's getting dark. You'd better go home."

To my surprise no one moved. "We don't care," someone called out. "Carry on!" All fear had left these people. Night after night, as they heard the word of God, faith rose within them. Eventually they would leave the tent in pitch darkness, singing hymns and choruses and praising God at the tops of their voices. Once again God showed me that it is signs and wonders that draw people to the Lord, especially when they are living in such desperate conditions. That is how Jesus worked, by showing the power of God in the miracles he performed.

Every evening the off-duty soldiers came to hear the gospel, and many of them found Jesus. The people of Magoda and Indaleni sat side by side, some visibly armed with revolvers. As we watched these men weeping before the Lord, we realised afresh that he was keeping us safe. Without permission from God, no one can touch his children.

The three weeks flew by. "Please don't go," the people begged. "There has been such peace here, and we have felt the presence of God. Please don't leave us."

One young man testified to the effect of our campaign. "This is the first time in months that I have been able to sleep peacefully," he said. "The peace of God has come here. I have been in the tent every night and seen people from both sides worshipping peacefully together, praying to one God."

I was sad to leave, too, but I knew it was the Lord's will that we hand over to the local ministers. I charged them to take care of the people. "They are your responsibility now," I said. "I have done what God called me to do, and now I call on you to keep the fires burning. Jesus will remain with you."

As we prayed the final benediction, the heavens opened and a mighty thunderstorm broke loose. There was so much rain that the water ran in rivers through the tent. There was no doubt that it was time for us to go! It felt like a sign from the Lord, sealing his blessing. These are rural people and they were jumping for joy: they had been planting their potatoes and maize in the dust for weeks. Now their crops would grow, and they were chanting, "Thank you, thank you, Jesus!" It was a wonderful climax to a special campaign.

We took the tent down on 20 November and it was a solemn occasion. Not one person had been murdered in the township during our time there, and we rejoiced at the goodness of God. Newspaper articles in the following weeks reported on the "miracle of peace" that had come to Richmond.

I knew that the problems of Richmond were repeated in townships all across Africa, and I burned to take God's peace to those places that were lost in darkness and violence. How could it be done? How could we take a tent this size around to all those distant places? We needed electricity supplies to run our lighting and loudspeaker systems. Where would we find the facilities we needed in rural areas, miles from the nearest town? I wrestled with this intractable problem, and handed it over to the Lord. I waited on him in prayer and hoped he would offer me a solution. Exactly three months later he gave me his answer.

11

The Seed Sower

*I*t was a Friday morning, 26 February 1999, and I was praying in my office, listening for God's guidance. His voice spoke clearly in my thoughts: "What are you doing with the seed I gave you, Angus?"

As a farmer, I know the importance of seed, and a picture formed in my mind. I imagined a great storehouse full of bags and bags of seed, lying in heaps and completely unused.

"This seed is the written word of God," the Lord said to me. "Africa needs my word."

Africa is my homeland and it has always been dear to my heart, but now I felt a new concern. I saw millions and millions of starving people crying out for help – and I knew the Lord was talking about more than physical hunger. Seed corn and seed potatoes could be planted to feed the body, but only the seed of God's word could feed the people with the bread of life. I had been preaching the gospel and running crusades for ten years, and I knew from experience how powerful the word of God is: it sets captives free, heals the broken-hearted and quickens new spiritual life.

The devil is working overtime in Africa. AIDS and malaria affect millions of people; illnesses which are trivial in other parts of the world kill the young and the elderly because they are weakened by hunger and poverty. Too often people who are desperate do not share what they have or care for one another: instead they grab what they can and lash out in anger and violence. The country is gripped by sin, corruption and poverty, so that the riches of its natural resources are wasted and aid fails to reach the needy. I began to realise afresh that the worst sickness of all is the spiritual darkness over the continent, because the light of God's word is not being shed abroad. There are churches and institutions, but no powerful testimony to the risen Lord: they are "having a form of godliness but denying its power" (2 Timothy 3:5).

We praise God for the missionaries and the Christian workers who are labouring faithfully in Africa, but still millions die every day without Christ.

"Lord, what can I do?" I asked.

"Plant the seed of my word, Angus."

I knew what to do with seed on my farm. If I had a huge field to sow, I would use a mechanical planter. With a machine like that it's possible to plant a lot of seed in a short time.

"This task is enormous," I said. "What I need is a seed sower."

"That's right," the Lord replied, "and this is what it looks like."

Immediately a picture came into my mind of an extraordinary vehicle: a massive 20-tonne, 4x4 Mercedes Benz truck, painted bright yellow, towing a huge trailer equipped with a platform, a big lighting plant and a powerful sound system. It was a mobile crusade system.

"Lord, this is wonderful!" I cried. "Instead of bringing people to the gospel campaigns, we take the campaigns to the people. We can go to the heart of Africa, where there are absolutely no facilities, where the gospel has never been preached. But why such a bright yellow?"

The answer came at once. "So that people can see it from miles away!" That made sense.

I was filled with excitement, and I couldn't wait to share the vision with the rest of the Shalom community. We had no idea where we would find such a vehicle or how we would finance it – we estimated that the budget for the project would be over a million Rand – but that didn't matter. William Carey, the great Baptist missionary, said, "Attempt great things for God and expect great things from God." My heart witnesses to that challenge. At Shalom we have a saying that if your vision doesn't scare you, it isn't big enough. This vision was big.

One of my heroes has always been David Livingstone. He had a passion for bringing Jesus Christ, the Light of the world, into darkest Africa, and even now his memory is revered. He is the only white man whose name remains in Africa north of the Limpopo River: while other place names were changed after independence, the town of Livingstone retains his name. Livingstone never saw his vision come to pass, but he sowed the good seed; his work led to the abolition of the slave trade and opened up the

African continent to the rest of the world. He has inspired countless Christians to preach the gospel. Now I had a vision that the Seed Sower would follow in his footsteps, bearing precious seed throughout Africa, and reaping where he sowed so many years ago.

I shared that vision wherever we went, and I talked about it when I spoke at a Men's Breakfast meeting in Richmond. Malcolm Anderson attended that meeting and he gave his heart to the Lord; two weeks later he telephoned me. "I've found the Seed Sower," he said.

I was stunned to find things happening so quickly; at that time I had only about R500 available.

"Don't worry about the price," said Malcolm. "Is it the right truck or not?"

The truck was perfect: it was a 1993 Mercedes Benz fire engine with only 40,000 kilometres on the clock. We had it painted bright yellow and dedicated it to the Lord. Then we were given an old eleven-metre trailer and Ian Miller, a Christian friend, rebuilt it. He cut it to size, removed the rust and rebuilt the suspension, and attached a portable platform to the side. A sound system and lights were built in, together with a generator and a 40-kilowatt lighting plant, capable of lighting up a small town.

We also added a 1,000-litre tank for drinking water: we were planning to travel into areas where cholera and other diseases are rife, and I knew fresh drinking water would be essential. The seven diesel tanks hold 2,500 litres of fuel, enough to take us from South Africa into the heart of the Congo without refuelling. It makes us virtually self-sufficient, and able to travel thousands of kilometres into the heart of the countryside; within 30 minutes of arriving we can be set up and ready to minister to the community.

Some of our Christian friends watched our preparations with interest. "Why does it have to be a Mercedes Benz?" they asked. "Surely something less expensive would do."

"That's the picture God gave me," I answered. Later I found out that the only type of truck that has spares readily available throughout Africa is the Mercedes Benz. The Lord certainly knows what he is doing – he is the God of detail indeed.

Our first trip was scheduled for June 2000, but various delays in equipping the truck held us back, and it was July before we were ready to leave. Only two of us – I and my engineer, Dirk – would take the Seed Sower into Zambia. There we would pick up the rest of the local team, including the musicians and an interpreter, Peter Mutale. Dirk was sitting in the truck with the engine running, but I stopped as I was about to climb into the cab.

"Wait a minute, Dirk," I called. "I won't be long." I went back up to the house to sit for a moment with Jill. It was always hard for me to leave the family, and this time was no exception. The children had all left home, and I knew Jill was going to be lonely. I took her hand in mine.

"Look after my wife, Lord," I prayed. "Keep her safe. You know what troubled times we live in, especially here in KwaZulu-Natal."

We held each other tightly as we said goodbye. Neither of us knew what lay ahead, except that there would be thousands of miles of distance between us. We had planned eleven crusades, back-to-back: I was facing six weeks with little or no contact with home. I would have to rely entirely on the Lord to take care of my loved ones. I thanked God for a precious wife who was willing to let me go about the Master's business.

We drove up the little farm road and out of the gate. It was the beginning of a journey that would take us six days and nights to reach the northernmost part of Zambia on the Congo border. We would travel to places that had never heard the gospel, and sow the seed of the word of God. What an honour.

We arrived safely in Zambia and assembled our team, and travelled on together. One of our crusades was at Kazembe, a big sprawling village of mud huts with thatched roofs. As we came over a rise in the road we could see a crowd of about 200 people completely blocking the road: from a distance it looked as if a riot was starting. We slowed down to see what they wanted, and realised that they were singing and dancing.

"They have come to greet us," said Peter Mutale.

The welcoming crowd escorted us right into the village, past the main shopping centre to a large football field. Dirk and the rest of the team got the big trailer set up as I prepared for the evening meeting. I wondered if David Livingstone had walked along these very streets. I had read his journal for 1867, when he met the chief of the Lunda tribe, a wicked man who traded in slaves stolen from weaker tribes, keeping them at Kazembe until Arab traders came to buy them. It was seeing the despair of the slaves, who often died on the forced march to the coast, that inspired Livingstone to campaign for the abolition of slavery.

That first night between 2,000 and 3,000 people came to the meeting. Hundreds responded to the altar call and accepted Jesus Christ as their Lord and Saviour. The people were so excited that they didn't want to go home – the only way we could get them to leave was by turning off the lights and plunging the field into darkness.

One of the heartening things was to see how hungry the people were for the word of God. When we distributed Bibles there was a huge rush to get them. Pastors who finally had a Bible of their own would clutch it to their chest, weeping. It was a challenge to those of us who have several Bibles gathering dust on our bookshelves.

That first night I was dozing off to sleep when I heard the drums start up, and I was reminded that however much enthusiasm for the gospel we saw at our meetings, we were surrounded by a pagan world. Peter Mutale had warned me as we approached the town.

"*Baba*," he said, "we have come at a very God-appointed time. This is one of the headquarters of witchcraft in the Luapula Valley, and the *Ntumbuka* ceremony is about to start. See those little huts on the bank of the river? They are for the water spirits to live in."

This ceremony is performed every year, when sacrifices are offered to address the ancestral spirits and appease the river gods. I realised suddenly that in spite of our frustration at the delay in starting our trip, God's timing had been perfect. We had been brought to the village just in time to confront the witchcraft and ancestor-worship which dominated the area.

In spite of the hundreds of drums echoing through the night in perfect unison, I fell asleep in confidence and peace. I knew we were surrounded by angels and upheld by the prayers of the saints. Whenever I preached I told the people that their ancestors and tribal spirits had no power over them; only the one true God, Creator of the world and Father of his people, could help them. When the villagers saw his power demonstrated in miracles of healing, thousands of them believed and turned their backs on the pagan ceremonies being conducted at the riverside.

It was a joy to me to see people rejecting witchcraft, and I thanked God for the privilege of bringing his word to this area. At the same time, I had struggles of my own: I was finding this crusade to be hard work. One of the problems was food: I was often hungry. The Zambian people are generous with what they have, but they are poor and they generally eat sparingly. Their diet consists of maize meal, cassava (a white root which is all starch and has very little nutritional value), spinach and sometimes a piece of very old, tough chicken. Other than the occasional boiled egg as a real treat or some rice, there is no variation in this diet, and I found it not only dull but often inadequate.

Our patience was also tested by the constant moving around from town to town, often camping but sometimes staying in a house. We used a bucket of water to wash in, and even if we had access to a bath, there would be no running water. Often we washed outside in the open or in the river. It was another adjustment to our lifestyle. These things may sound trivial, but when they go on for weeks they can be very trying, and add to the general stress.

I was homesick for my wife and family, and for the familiar scenes of my home: I am deeply attached to the land the Lord has given me to farm and live in, and when I am away from it I feel the separation keenly.

I also missed being alone. I'm not used to having people around me all the time, but here, from first light until last thing at night when we turned off the lighting plant, swarms of little children hung around the Seed Sower. There were people there continually, night and day.

David Livingstone had the same experience. He was forced to draw a circle in the sand with a stick and seat himself inside, and no one was allowed to cross the line while he ate his meals. That was the only peace he could get from the milling crowds. I knew exactly how he felt. I tried to imitate him by making a circle round the Seed Sower with red and white tape, but it didn't work so well for me. Five minutes later the children were all inside the circle, peering into the truck. They were precious little souls who needed Jesus and I loved every one of them, but I decided the Lord was using them to strip me of every ounce of independence and privacy.

Whenever I was tempted to start complaining, though, I thought of what Jesus went through for us. "Foxes have holes and birds of the air have nests, but the Son of Man has nowhere to lay his head" (Matthew 8:20). He was constantly surrounded by large crowds of people and had to go up into the mountain to be alone. He too was often hungry. I wrote in my journal, "Lord Jesus, thank you for seeing fit to use me. Don't allow me to let you down, I pray. I intend to finish these eleven campaigns at any cost."

We were packing up to leave when a Zambian pastor came up to me. "Brother Angus," he said, "do you see that fig tree at the bottom of the field?"

"Yes, I see it," I replied.

"Do you know that David Livingstone camped there when he came to Kazembe?"

My heart skipped a beat. We were truly travelling in the footsteps of Livingstone. I ran across the field and stood under the tree for a moment, thanking the Lord for the privilege of being there. I praised him for all the people who had stood up for him each night of our crusade, and prayed that he would strengthen them to keep the faith and continue in their walk with Jesus.

Livingstone wrote in his journals that he was ploughing and preparing the soil. Although he led few to Christ, he believed that others would come after him and reap a mighty crop. All he asked was that we never cease to remember those who went before us. Those thousands who came forward at Kazembe are part of that crop, and the scripture in Hebrews comes to mind: "Therefore, since we are surrounded by such a great cloud of witnesses, let us throw off everything that hinders and the sin that so easily entangles, and let us run with perseverance the race marked out for us" (Hebrews 12:1). I am sure David Livingstone was standing up in heaven with tears running down his face as he saw that mighty harvest coming in.

At the end of our six-week journey we turned our faces towards home, thanking God for the work that he had done. The Seed Sower had proved itself over and over again, bringing us safely along rough and damaged roads and making it possible to minister to people deep in the countryside, in rural communities far from the cities. We were happy when we finally arrived back at the farm, and joyfully recounted our adventures to the rest of the team at Shalom.

A year later we set off again, travelling to Zambia and Tanzania. This time we didn't bother to take clothes or food as gifts for the people, but only Christian literature and Bibles. We had realised that the people were only interested in the word of God; by the end of our first crusade we had given away 16,500 gospels of John and huge quantities of other Christian literature.

I was accompanied on this journey by my nephew Fraser, and I thanked God for this anointed young man who has Africa in his heart. I thanked him, too, for the faith of my brother Fergus, who had entrusted his son to my care, having already lost little Alistair in that terrible accident. Fraser didn't have a driving licence, so his contribution was to handle the sound system, the lighting, the cooking and all the other odd jobs. His faith was growing in maturity all the time, and he came home from our trip with a strong desire to dedicate his life to full-time service, preaching the gospel of Jesus Christ in Africa.

We were on a tight schedule, and hoping to catch the last ferry across the mighty Zambezi River so that we could cross over to Zambia. However, God had other plans. We arrived too late and were forced to spend the night on the Botswana side of the border, along with lots of other trucks making the long-distance journey. We had plenty of time to get talking to their drivers, who came from all over Africa: the Congo, Zambia, Botswana, South Africa and Zimbabwe. We told them about our truck, which has just one word, "Jesus", painted in black on the side.

"Do you have any Bibles?" they asked. We opened our boxes and started handing them out freely. Every one was a seed of God's word, and who knew what fruit it would bear? Just then another driver approached us.

"Excuse me," he said, "my name is Gabriel. I have a question to ask you. What must a man do to be saved?"

We were so excited. Here was a man asking the same question that has been asked so many times over the centuries, like Nicodemus who asked it of Jesus (John 3:4), the eunuch who met Philip when riding in his chariot (Acts 8:31), or the jailer who asked it of Paul and Silas (Acts 16:30).

"You must be born again," we told him, and explained how he too could accept Jesus into his life. Right there among all those tough truck drivers, on the banks of the Zambezi, Gabriel bowed his head and prayed the sinner's prayer with us. It set the seal of God's blessing on our journey.

We had some wonderful meetings in Zambia. In Mbala around a thousand people surrendered their lives to the Lord; the personal representative of President Frederick Chiluba and his adviser for the Northern Province were there, and they both made a public commitment to Jesus. Three meetings in Kasama brought 750 responses. In Mpulungu, northern Zambia, at the foot of Lake Tanganyika, we saw 2,000 people accept the Lord. Fraser had his heart set on being baptised in Central Africa and I had the privilege of baptising him there in the clear waters of Lake Tanganyika.

We crossed Malawi and entered southern Tanzania, heading for the town of Mtwara, close to the coast and the northern border of Mozambique. The road was very rough, and the trip took us four days. We passed six broken-down trucks on the way, but the Seed Sower rolled safely on, without even a puncture.

Mtwara is a town of 40,000 people, and they had never had a gospel crusade before. It is in a rural area, steeped in witchcraft. A powerful spirit called a *geni* is invoked on all babies when they are born, and children are sometimes offered to the gods as human sacrifices. When girls reach puberty they may be offered on an auction block to the highest bidder. At the time of the *Ngoma* ceremony, held every year, men will sell everything they have in order to buy alcohol for the celebrations that last for several weeks.

We arrived late, so there was only time for two of the three meetings we had planned. The local clergy informed us that we would not be able to preach until the next day, when we could obtain formal permission from the authorities. We would be risking jail if we preached without permission.

We decided we wouldn't be put off: we had travelled 8,000 kilometres to get there, and we were going ahead, even if it meant going to prison. We put up the platform, switched on the lights and began the service. In this coastal area Islam is very strong, and we could see a group of Muslim men at the side of the crowd, watching closely to see who made a decision for Christ. The people were silent and there seemed to be an atmosphere of great fear and oppression.

"Let's sing," I said. As we began to praise God, an amazing change came over the people. They started singing and dancing in a circle, and the dust rose in thick clouds from the beating of their feet. The loudspeakers were at full volume and the atmosphere changed to one of joy.

I stood up to preach, but there seemed to be little response. Then I recalled something Jill had said to me. On the way to Mtwara I had telephoned her from a local missionary's home.

"Angus," she told me, "the intercessors have had a word from the Lord. God says, 'Don't restrict the children.'"

As I looked down at the crowd in front of me, I could see hundreds of little street children struggling to get to the front. Some of the organisers were hitting their legs with sticks to keep them back.

"Leave them alone!" I called. "Let them come." An absolute wave of children came surging forward, and behind them came the grown-ups. The resistance to the ministry melted away, and from that moment I could feel the Holy Spirit being freed to move among the people.

The next day we had another wonderful meeting. Many people responded to the altar call, but I could see several of the local pastors hanging back in the crowd, unwilling to come forward. I became very angry.

"I'm talking to you, too," I said. "If you love Jesus, I challenge you to raise your hands so everyone can see who you are. We need to lead from the front. This is your finest hour. If the shepherds are afraid to identify themselves, what are the sheep to do?"

One by one they raised their hands, and once again the whole atmosphere lifted. When the word of God is preached in power, an anointing comes upon the people. However much the local Christians may be cowed by witchcraft, sin or immorality, they change when they begin to experience the power of God. Now those pastors broke branches from the trees and waved them enthusiastically as they sang and danced in praise of the Lord.

Then a Muslim man walked up to the Seed Sower in front of everyone. He took the *taqiyah*, his white Islamic cap, from his head and threw it onto the platform.

"Burn it," he said. "From today I am going to follow Jesus."

Fraser and I packed up the truck that evening with joy in our hearts, and when we said our goodbyes the next day we felt we were leaving friends behind us.

"We'll be back," we promised them, and we trust we will be able to fulfil that promise. There is so much work to be done.

God has called us to take the Seed Sower and

spread his word in Africa. Our commission is to be the light of the world, and I truly believe that the old description of Africa as the "Dark Continent" is going to change. Already this land is beginning to send great preachers and evangelists all over the world, especially into the nations of the developed world where the riches of the consumer society are encouraging people to serve other gods.

Africa still suffers today from the influence of the occult, ancestor-worship, witchcraft, immorality, corruption, greed, AIDS, poverty and disregard for human life. By the grace of God we, as children of the living Christ, are following in the footsteps of Livingstone, and taking the seed of God's word and sowing it in every corner of the land. We are trusting God for nothing less than a Holy Spirit revival in Africa.

12
Going Forward

*D*avid Livingstone said, "I will go anywhere, as long as it is forward." That is how we feel at Shalom. There is so much work to be done before the Lord returns, that there is no time to sit back and relax. We are going forward.

I am amazed at what the Lord has done in my life, and how far the gospel can reach when it is faithfully preached.

In 2001 I was invited to make a five-week tour of New Zealand. For part of the time Jill was with me, which was a wonderful bonus. We travelled extensively throughout the North and South Islands, and found it one of the most beautiful countries we had ever seen. I spoke to people in churches, farmers' meetings, schools and colleges. I was particularly excited about sharing the gospel with the Maori people.

The Maoris are a beautiful and charming people, but they are very defensive about their culture and native religion, a position I can understand. I too come from a place where culture is important. Yet adhering to that culture has brought problems: in Africa it is traditional among the tribes for a man to take a young girl to his bed before he marries. That tradition has opened the way for AIDS to attack a whole generation. The gospel, however, transcends culture: in New Zealand as in Africa we stressed that there is only one God, and he alone is to be served and worshipped in holiness of life and moral purity. Like many other New Zealanders the Maoris felt that there was more to life than they were experiencing, and they were open to receive the message of new life that we brought. We saw miraculous healings testifying to the power of the one God, and many of them believed.

Later that year a farmer from England came to see me. His name was David Harper, and he had been given a copy of the earlier South African edition of *Faith Like Potatoes*.

"The British farmers need you to come and speak to them, Angus," he told me. He spoke to our fellowship at Shalom: "Please release this man for three weeks. God needs him in England." He had held an all-night prayer meeting on his farm, and his friends felt so strongly that we should visit England that they opened their wallets and put money down on the kitchen table to pay for the campaign.

When I went to England in February 2002 I found the English farmers disillusioned and depressed. A series of disasters – the epidemic of bovine spongiform encephalitis ("mad cow disease"), foot-and-mouth disease, and then a winter of terrible flooding – had driven many to desperation. David's inspired advertising poster for our Healing the Land campaign showed a picture of cows being burned on a farm. It read, "Is farming killing you? Need some answers?

Then be at the Corn Exchange, Newbury, and hear one man's amazing story."

We saw some wonderful miracles during that campaign as money and venues were made available, enabling us to preach the gospel as we travelled across England and Wales. Hundreds of people were healed, gave their lives to the Lord and found new hope and new life in him.

Over the last 16 years we have held more than 200 major campaigns all over South Africa, Zimbabwe, Zambia, Mozambique, Tanzania, Botswana, Kenya, England, Scotland, Wales, Australia and New Zealand. In the summer of 2005 we made our longest-yet journey with the Seed Sower, taking 200,000 gospels to Uganda.

There is work to be done in South Africa, too, and our team is growing. When our little prayer chapel became too small for our Sunday fellowship, I knew I didn't have the money to rebuild.

"It will just have to wait a while," I said to Jill.

Fortunately my wife continually challenges me with the word of God.

"We've trusted God in the past and he's never let us down," she reminded me. "How come we can't trust him now for a new building?"

After much thought and prayer, I took her good counsel.

"Right, we'll step out in faith," I told the team. "We often have large gatherings here, so if we're going to build an auditorium, let's do it properly."

I rang a good friend in the building industry. "How much would it cost to build an auditorium to seat around 700 people?" I asked. He promised to get me a quotation. A little while later he rang me back: he had a steel structure that would do for the auditorium, and he was willing to give it to us as a gift. He also had the corrugated iron for the roof, the window frames and the paint for the whole thing. All we had to do was put the walls up.

Now we have a wonderful centre for large meetings, with a platform, and lighting and sound systems, built by faith and the generosity of the fellowship, and all the praise and glory goes to our Lord Jesus Christ. This summer it was the centre for our Mighty Men conference. I have been praying for years for revival in this country, and this year God gave me a taste of what he has in store for us.

Over 600 men from all over Africa attended – leaders from the fields of commerce, industry, agriculture, sport and education. These are men with power and influence in our continent, successful in their lives, but all acknowledging their need for the Lord to guide and direct them. Our theme was taken from 2 Corinthians 5:17-20: "Therefore, if anyone is in Christ, he is a new creation; the old has gone, the new has come! All this is from God, who reconciled us to himself through Christ and gave us the ministry of reconciliation: that God was reconciling the world to himself in Christ, not counting men's sins against them. And he has committed to us the message of reconciliation. We are therefore Christ's ambassadors, as though God were making his appeal through us. We implore you on Christ's behalf: Be reconciled to God."

When you mention reconciliation in South Africa,

all too often you see the shutters come down: it has been the same cry for years. However, we were no longer talking about reconciliation between black and white, but between fathers and sons, between brothers and between churches. I had been preaching all afternoon on this theme when I had a word from the Lord.

"There are two people here who need to make up their differences," I said. "A man and his son. I appeal to you to be reconciled in Christ."

There was a moment of silence, and then two men got to their feet. They were sitting on opposite sides of the hall, which tells you something about their relationship, that they could attend the same conference and manage to keep that distance between them. They walked towards each other and met in the centre aisle, where they hugged each other. People were in tears as they watched. That opened the floodgates, and for three hours we had people coming forward and confessing their sins to each other. Two young men got up and confessed to their father, "We told Mum that she had to leave you. You treated her so badly." The father embraced them and asked their forgiveness for what he had done to destroy their family life.

A father came to the microphone and spoke to his son, somewhere in the audience. "I'm sorry, son, that I never told you that you were good enough, that I love you and I'm proud of you." A boy of about 18 stood up; he ran up the aisle and into his father's arms.

We discovered that we had members of not one but two separate churches which had each been split down the middle by disagreements; they were reconciled and pledged to go forward in unity once more. As always, I could only stand and watch in awe as the power of God was manifested in the crowd before me. I felt like Robert Murray McShane, the Scottish evangelist, who said, "Rather than being an instrument of the Lord, all I was, was an adoring spectator."

The auditorium enables us to continue holding events like this at the farm, and people love to spend time there at the heart of the Shalom ministry.

It is many years since I handed over the farming side of my work to my sons, and they have made a great success of it. At the time I was visiting a little farming community in the southern tip of the Cape, and I stayed with a local family. The father had bought the farm for his three sons, and thought that they would plant crops and buy livestock; he was astonished when they told him that they had other ideas. They let the land revert to its natural state, which we call *fynbos* – open land producing the most wonderful array of wild flowers. They are now the largest employers in the area, with a fleet of trucks and a flourishing export business, supplying the world with South African wild flowers. Their success is all because their father was not too proud to listen to his sons, and released the farm into their capable hands.

One of the brothers turned to me and asked about my farm. I was happy to tell him about the business I loved so much.

"How old are your sons?" he asked. "What are their qualifications?" I realised that not only was Andrew older than I had been when I started farming, but he was also a great deal better qualified!

"When are you going to give your sons an opportunity to farm for themselves?" he asked, and the Holy Spirit opened my heart and showed me that he was right. That night I telephoned Andy and said, "When you are ready, the farm is waiting for you."

He is a godly young man and said, "Thank you, Dad, I'll pray about it." Two years later he came home, and now he and Fergus are running the farms between them. It's a joy to come home from a long preaching campaign, saddle up my horse and ride through the farms to see the work my sons have done. I know the Lord is as proud of them as I am. At the same time, the ministry which the Lord has given to me is flourishing.

I have also released the pastoral work at Shalom to Marc and Mandy Porée, a gifted young couple who live on the farm with their children, Emma and Caleb. Marc has been visiting Shalom since his schooldays, a spiritual son from those early youth meetings I led. They are involved in organising outreach in our local area, and they have trained a team of evangelists who visit local schools, hospitals and homes for the elderly.

All the family are involved in some way with our work at Shalom. Andrew had a successful farming career in Mozambique before he came home to take over the farm. He is married to Rochelle and they have two lovely children, Kyla and Jaimee. Lindi is married to Paul Praschma, and they live in Durban with their son Kai; they are both Christians and uphold us with their prayers and loving support. Our daughter Robyn is a beautiful child of God, and she uses her many talents to the full, acting as our music leader, teaching at Halalisani School and running

Beth Hatlaim, our children's home. Fergus works the farm with Andy; a sportsman who has a gift with horses, he is our stockman. Jilly, our youngest, is now married to Greg Hull, a Christian farmer from Greytown. Their wedding was held at Shalom, a beautiful family affair with all the smallest boys wearing kilts like me! Jilly is still the nurse for Beth Hatlaim.

My brother Fergus always said that when he retired he was coming to Shalom to carry my Bible for me; in fact he organises our campaigns for us. His wife Joanne is our bookkeeper and his son Fraser is my "Timothy" – my protégé and an effective preacher in his own right.

Jill, meanwhile, is my strength and mainstay, an intercessor who loves to spend time in prayer. There are no words for what I owe her. "A wife of noble character who can find? She is worth far more than rubies ... Her children arise and call her blessed; her husband also, and he praises her: 'Many women do noble things, but you surpass them all'" (Proverbs 31:10, 28, 29).

Everyone who lives in our community at Shalom is part of our family, from Peggy and Moyra, our elderly prayer warriors, to the youngest child in the children's home. I believe that family is closer to God's heart than anything else, the support system he has given us to build us up in faith, and to support us when we falter. If we want our family lives to conform to God's will, Jesus must be our priority, our focal point, in our homes as well as in our ministries.

That doesn't mean that it's always easy to live together: home can be the hardest place to live a

Christian life. That's where people see us when we're tired and our defences are down. I find life much easier when I'm out on the road preaching the gospel – when I'm at home people see me as I really am. Home is the place where God moulds us and teaches us unselfishness and caring in the humdrum reality of everyday work.

An agricultural setting is a wonderful place for ironing out impatience, bad temper, selfishness and jealousy, and teaching us to depend on God for the strength to build character. There is nothing like a farm for bringing us back to basics and making us see how helpless we are before God. There have been many times when drought has threatened and we have gone into our little chapel and prayed together as a community. From the smallest child to the oldest of our residents, everybody knows that if it doesn't rain we need to call on God together, and to do that we first have to put aside our differences. "Leave your gift there in front of the altar. First go and be reconciled to your brother; then come and offer your gift" (Matthew 5:24). A family that prays together stays together: we believe that and we practise it.

One thing that God has laid on my heart is the importance of having order in the family. First, the Lord Jesus takes pre-eminence. Everything follows from that. The father is the head of the home; the mother is the heart of the home; the children are the reward, the joy and the life of the home. The same is true of the extended family. My role as the head of the family is a responsibility. I may not just do as I please at Shalom: I am accountable to everyone, from the oldest to the youngest. We pray together about things, I take counsel from everybody, and then I go to God and pray, and he shows me what I have to do. I believe that is the way God intends it to be, and many ministries which degenerate into failure and scandal do so because there is no accountability.

I once heard a man say, "It is because of my wife and children that I have to live a holy life." There is truth in that. I dare not fall short of what God has called me to for the sake of the gospel and for my family and loved ones. There is a built-in security in belonging to a family, especially the family of God.

We often spend time with our youngest children, telling them the stories of Shalom; how we got started; how we built the first house out of wattle and daub; how we had to dig a hole in the ground to find water; how we had to pull up the trees one by one to make the fields where we plant our crops; how we won the Grand Championship with our first ox. They love to hear those stories, and as they hear them, they learn to trust the God who rewards his faithful people with his blessing.

Our farm workers also know that our strength is in the Lord. On the farm we pray, sing hymns and read the scriptures regularly. I was challenged to do this when I observed the faithfulness of the Muslim community: they pray to a god with whom they do not have a personal relationship, yet they close down their businesses every Friday for an hour of prayer. We serve the living God: surely we can give him an hour of our time!

So every Wednesday morning from ten to eleven

we stop all our work. We stop the maize mill, call all the staff from the far corners of the farm (this takes far longer than an hour!) and meet in the chapel. There we praise and worship God, and we do it in our time, not our workers' time.

The results have been amazing. We have experienced an incredible turnaround in relationships, and an improvement in the working atmosphere on the farm in general. There is power in prayer. When men work, they work. But when men pray, God works. Our country has been through terrible times, and there are legacies of anger and resentment everywhere. I thank God that by his grace he has placed a spirit of forgiveness in people's hearts, joining the community at Shalom into one family, black and white together.

They say that someone once asked Martin Luther, "If you knew the Lord was coming tomorrow, what would you do?" He replied, "I'd plant another apple tree." That is how we are going forward at Shalom: carrying on in love and trust in the Lord, doing his will until he comes.

When I look around me I am astonished at what the Lord has done. I am a simple farmer, an ordinary man with very little education, and yet today I find myself involved in TV programmes, radio programmes, gospel campaigns, running a children's home and managing a school, writing books and travelling the world. However much I have travelled, and however much my life has changed, I have never moved far from Shalom, my roots. The farm is the backbone of my ministry, and it's often the passport that gets me into places. A pastor in a dog-collar wouldn't be invited to half the places I visit, from farmers' meetings to prisons. It's because I'm a man of the soil, an ordinary man who knows what it is to do a long day's hard manual labour, that doors have opened and people have listened to what I have to say. I have been able to introduce them to the one who was truly Man, who knows all about our troubled humanity, and who stands beside us as our Friend and Lord.

Preaching the gospel can be emotionally demanding and physically tiring, yet I am committed to doing the Lord's will, to the best of my ability. I notice this especially when I'm away from home on a long trip, perhaps travelling for long hours in difficult terrain, or surrounded by hundreds of people for weeks on end. Far away from the loving support of my wife and family, and the peace and solitude of the farm, I am made to realise over again that we have only one source of strength: the Lord himself.

It is impossible to hear from God unless we spend time with him. The Bible tells us that Jesus often went up into the mountain to be with his Father, even during his busiest and most critical times. He returned filled with power. I have found that the more time I spend with God, the more clearly I hear from him. I don't mean that God speaks to me audibly; but he speaks to me through the wonders of creation, the clouds and sun and rain, through the wisdom of my praying friends and in the quietness of my spirit. When I spend time with God, my way becomes clear.

At home I go to my office or out into the fields to be alone. I read the Bible, often a portion from the Old Testament and one from the New Testament, and I make a note of what the Lord has told me in his word. When I look back at those notes they often astonish me: time and time again he has given me sermons to preach, answers to decisions I have to make, or new directions to explore.

When I have finished reading the scriptures, I begin to pray. I thank the Lord for every gift he has given me, and those good things he is going to give me. I pray for my family and loved ones, for friends, and for their needs. It's only after spending as long as possible in prayer that I go out to do my day's work. I come out of that quiet time spent with God with peace in my spirit and clarity in my thoughts, enabling me to preach with confidence that the message is his.

Often when I am away from home in a city or a crowded airport, I feel hemmed in by buildings and people, unable to let my spirit expand as it does in the wide open spaces of the farm. How can one find peace in a hectic day? I read somewhere that many Russian Christians have a little hide-away at the bottom of their gardens where they go to spend time with God; it's called a *postinia*. Then I heard an international speaker say that God had given him a *postinia* in his mind, a place he could retreat to in the midst of a crowd and be quiet. I realised that was exactly what I needed.

When I am on the road and ministering to hundreds of people, with all their needs and concerns weighing heavily on my heart, I retreat into my *postinia*. I sit quietly and close my eyes and picture a beautiful scene – the mountains of Scotland or the maize fields of Shalom. As my mind and my spirit quieten, I can speak to God and listen to him. I tell the Lord how much I love him, I ask him to protect my family, and I thank him for the blessing of his love. I ask for strength, for help to be more single-minded and focused on the mission set before me, crying out for more compassion for lost souls. I ask him to show me how to put aside my own desires and to live for him alone. That is when the love of God seems to fill my soul. Jesus has never let me down.

If you have never known the Lord Jesus Christ in this way, I beg you to repent and ask God to forgive you and renew your relationship with him. You will only really believe that the Lord can work a miracle in your life if you know him. If you don't know the Lord, it doesn't matter how much other people tell you about him, you will never really trust him until you know him personally.

I would like to challenge whoever is reading this book to allow the Lord to lead you. If you know in your heart that you have never made a personal commitment to Christ, I encourage you to pray this prayer out loud. Afterwards, tell three people what you have done: it is very important to make a public confession of your faith, so that it is firmly set in your heart.

The sinner's prayer
Dear Lord Jesus, I repent of all my sin.
I ask you to forgive me for not serving you with
   all my heart.
From this day forward I will start all over again.
And so, as I repent of every sin I have ever
   committed,

I ask you to come into my life, and to be the Lord
of my life.
I will serve no other God but you.
Thank you, Lord, that you are a covenant-keeping
God,
and even as I endeavour, by the power of your
Holy Spirit,
to keep my side of the covenant,
I know that you will keep your side.
I ask all these things in the powerful and precious
name of Jesus Christ,
my Lord and Saviour.
Amen.

Perhaps you wish to enter full-time service with Jesus
Christ, and dedicate your life to his ministry, but have
never taken that final step of faith. If you desire to
serve Jesus with all your heart, please pray this prayer,
and expect him to call you.

Prayer of dedication to full-time service
Dear Lord Jesus, I have given my life to you, but I
repent right now, because I have done very little
which is constructive for the kingdom of God. I ask
you to forgive me.

From today onwards I am offering myself for
full-time service. I acknowledge that the time is
short, that the kingdom of God is at hand, and that
people need to hear the gospel and repent.

There are so few people preaching the Good
News of Christ, although many are perishing
because they have never heard, and I want to make

a difference. I pray that you will use me in whatever area you are calling me to.

Help me to make a start after I have put this book down. Help me reach my next-door neighbour, the people down the street, and press right on as you lead. And, Lord, if you should call me to a foreign country, I pray that you will make a way for me and give me the faith and courage to follow it through. I ask this in Jesus' precious name. Amen.

If you have been blessed and challenged by this book and have prayed either – or both – of these prayers, please write and tell me about it at

Shalom Ministries
PO Box 373
Greytown
KwaZulu-Natal
South Africa 3250
www.shalomtrust.co.za